FUEL

BY

H G TUDOR

Fuel

By

H G Tudor

Published by Insight Books

Dedications

To the appliances. May you always remain efficient and productive.

All hail the Hoover.

Introduction

I am a narcissist and I am providing you with unrivalled insight into the very thing that we exist for. The holy grail of our reason for being here. The central core to our existence. Nowhere else will you gain such an insight into the behaviour of someone like me along with those of our kind. You may find parts of reading this uncomfortable. I offer no apology (of course you will be used to that) for that being the case. I do not wrap up what I write in euphemism or shirk from telling you precisely why my kind and me do as we do. You need to know this and you will find it easier to comprehend (even if it leaves you aghast) when it is delivered to you in a straight fashion.

You may be aware that you are in a relationship with a narcissist. If so, you have made a sensible step in reading this book to learn about what drives him or her on. This understanding will not only enable you to make sense of things which mystified you before, but it will also provide you with the opportunity to take steps to protect yourself. There are ways of managing and dealing with the narcissist that you have become entangled with.

You may not realise you are doing the dance with the narcissist. You may have reached this book through recommendation, or the blurb intrigued you or you might just have found the cover enticing. I should imagine however that is likely that you find yourself engaged in a relationship with someone (be it familial, intimate, a friend or work-related) and you cannot make sense of his or her behaviour. You apply logic to ascertaining why people act in the way that they do. You approach matters in a rational fashion and as a consequence you are perplexed at the behaviour that you are witnessing. That is understandable. Whilst we are methodical and scheming we do not operate to the same value systems as you. We do not reside in the same world as you since we create a different world where we rule and the rules are we. The application of rational thought will not help you solve the problem that you face. Reading this book and my other titles will give you the insight that you require so that you are able to make sense of what you are dealing with. Thus armed with this knowledge you are able to take the appropriate action.

I have heard all the plaintive questions before. Why are they so charming one day and so horrible the next? Why do they boast and seek compliments so frequently? Why do they appear to be at war with the world, always provoking arguments and seeking to upset people? How on earth can somebody live like that? Surely they can see that it is not a pleasant way to live? Surely they must wonder why they lose friends, lose jobs and are not invited by people to social events? Why must they behave like that?

The answer comes down to one word; fuel. It is all about the fuel. Fuel is what we must have and it is this precious commodity that is the root cause of the bizarre behaviour that you witness and indeed that affects you, often at a terrible cost to you. The individual who you have become enmeshed with, is in all likelihood a narcissist and they need fuel like you need the air that you breathe. By reading and understanding what this fuel is and the role it plays, you will begin to understand why this person acts this way and what you might do about it.

What is fuel? If you regard the word in its sense as a noun it is a material that is burned to produce heat or power. Expanding on this, one would regard fuel as those materials that store potential energy in forms that can be practicably released and used for work or as heat energy. There are many types of fuel. The oldest and most obvious is wood. The combustion of wood by our ancestors occurred around two million years ago. From that moment we have developed fuels to warm and to cook.

After that, fuel became required to power. Wood, peat and dung were all burned. Coal arrived and was used by the Chinese but when the British developed the steam engine, coal became more widely used as a power source. Coal drove ships and locomotives and its gas was used for street lighting. Thereafter, coal was used to generate electricity. Gaseous fuels such as hydrogen and propane have been developed. Liquid fuels have revolutionised transport and created massive wealth through diesel, kerosene and gasoline.

Biofuels have been developed and then nuclear fuel, which can be 'burned' by fission or fusion to create nuclear energy. Food is a fuel. We need it to sustain us as human beings. All around you and I is the need for fuel. The world demands more and more fuel and entire industries exist in the development of new fuels, the extraction of existing ones and increasing the efficiency of them also. Fuel is central to humankind's existence. Without fuel we will starve, become cold and lose an array of comforts, entertainments, services and necessities that are all made possible through the provision of fuel. It is absolutely fundamental to our existence. This is even more so with regard to the existence of my kind and me.

Accordingly, fuel as a noun is central to the world's population. That is its importance.

It is central to my kind and me. Without it, we too would not survive. I am not talking about food, coal or gasoline. I am referring to the fuel that the narcissist requires each and every day. It is perhaps even better understood by considering fuel as a verb.

'To cause (a fire) to burn more intensely'

We need fuel. We need to fuel the fire that burns inside of us. Fuel as a noun and as a verb is critical to us. It is absolutely essential. You need air to breathe. We need our fuel to exist and prosper. I cannot emphasise just how crucial fuel is to my kind and me. Accordingly, I am going to share with you my direct and forthright observations as to what our fuel is. Why do we need it? How do we gather it? What is your role in the provision of this fuel? How do we approach the harvesting of fuel? What are out methodologies? Why do we act in a certain way because of the need for fuel? How are others affected by our demands for fuel? To understand what our fuel is and why we need it in such voracious quantities is to better understand the narcissist. It will also enable you to fathom out why you are such an attraction to the narcissist and possibly what you may be able to do to change that. Understanding our relationship with fuel is central to understanding how a narcissist operates and exists. Above all we abide by the concept that fuel is the rule.

What is our fuel?

There is the concept of narcissistic supply. I suspect you will be familiar with this phrase. This is regarded as a type of admiration, interpersonal support or sustenance drawn by an individual from his or her environment and essential to their self-esteem. I understand that somebody called Otto Fenichel developed the concept. That appears to be the technical way that it is regarded. I prefer to call it fuel, not only is the word fuel more appropriate in terms of what it does for me, it is easier to type than keep repeating narcissistic supply. As, you know by now, I am all about looking at ways of saving energy.

People read the phrase 'narcissistic supply' and I know they will automatically attach a prejudicial label to the phrase because they have seen the word 'narcissistic'. This immediately conjures up connotations of selfishness, entitlement, haughtiness and a lack of caring about anyone else. By replacing narcissistic supply with the word 'fuel' we create a less prejudicial approach to understanding what it is that I need. We also do the same in understanding what you need. Yes, you need fuel as well. You see, if I suggested that you needed narcissistic supply, I should imagine that many of you would shake your heads and deny that to be the case.

"I am no narcissist," I hear you protest, "Why would I then need narcissistic supply?"

I understand your reluctance to be associated with anything that concerns my kind and me and therefore let us use fuel instead. Fuel makes us all feel good. I discuss in greater detail below the types of fuel that my kind and me require, but let's remain with the idea that you need fuel as well. You need people to provide you with love, with praise and approval.

You like somebody to say things such as: -

"I like the way you have done your hair."

"Great presentation you gave yesterday."

"That's a fantastic new car you've got there."

"Hey, I really like your bag, where can I get one?"

"I think you did really well dealing with that angry customer."

"I am always impressed by how claim you are in a difficult situation."

"You know so much about Thailand, I am planning a trip there and I
wondered if you could help me?"

Consider all those comments and you would readily admit that they are
regarded as pleasant things to say to someone else and the recipient will feel
better about themselves for hearing such a comment. This is fuel.
Everybody needs fuel and everybody consumes fuel. You and I are similar
in that regard.

Where we differ is by virtue of the fact that my kind and me need
vast quantities of this fuel. It is our sole pre-occupation in our lives. We are
insatiable in our desire to receive it. You, as a normal person, see no such
need to receive such large quantities of fuel. Indeed, should you be
subjected to such sustained supplies of fuel for a long period of time you
actually feel uncomfortable with it. I find that strange but I know that you
and I are very different creatures.

Moreover, we need this fuel repeatedly and often. We are unable to
go for long without gathering it and by long I mean hours. You on the other
hand have such self-sufficiency that you are able, as a normal person, to
endure a considerably lengthy period (several days, a week and beyond)
without having to receive such fuel. Small and intermittent amounts of fuel

are entirely satisfactory to you. I explain in greater detail why it is that we need such massive and frequent amounts of fuel. You might also note a further difference in this paragraph. I make mention of how you receive fuel and how my kind and me gather it. For you, the receipt of fuel is a passive process. You do not seek it out. It is pleasant when you receive it but you have no overriding desire (at least nowhere near the level at which we desire it) to have it. By contrast, we not only must receive it but we must hunt it out, harvest it and gather it.

A further distinction is the methodology applied to obtaining this fuel. As a normal person you do not seek to elicit the provision of this fuel. Its provision arises as a happy consequence of you providing something worthwhile or doing something to please yourself, which is noted by others. Considering the content of the sentences above, demonstrates how this is the case.

You have your hair done at the hairdresser so you feel smart and attractive. You have done this for yourself. You have not done it to impress anyone else. It is a pleasant side effect that others notice this and compliment you on it.

You have worked hard at ensuring that the presentation you will later give is accurate, helpful and that it will be well received. You are obliged to do this by virtue of your job or perhaps because you are engaged in some form of study. You want to ensure that you perform well in order to assert your self-worth and to avoid letting people down with a poor presentation. As a normal person, you will not have thought,
"I must do a great presentation so everyone will applaud and tell me how wonderful I am."
That is the way that my kind and me would regard the situation.

You bought a new car because you needed one and decided to reward yourself. You have a fashionable handbag for similar reasons. Others notice this and pass admiring comments. Often you have no need of expensive material possessions because you draw a sense of well-being from different things, such as the giving of your time or the provision of your compassion. You feel good about those comments but you did nothing to try and elicit them. The praise you received from handling an irate customer is a pleasant side effect from you demonstrating your people skills and carrying out your job.

Accordingly, the fuel that you obtain is all as a side-product of you doing other things. For us, the harvesting of the fuel is the sole reason for doing things.

I buy a new motor vehicle because I want people to: -

1.   See how well I am doing and admire me;
2.   Recognise what a great vehicle it is and admire me for owning it;
3.   Be envious of my ownership because my car is better than theirs;
4.   Demonstrate that by owning a better car I am superior to them.

All of this generates fuel for me. You ought to notice how the ways in which I obtain this fuel are greater in number that the way you would and that my fuel is based on both positive and negative reactions. I apply myself to securing those reactions. You do not.

Thus whilst we both like fuel, you do not need it in any where near the same way we do, nor do you set out to gather it in the way that we do.

Whilst Herr Fenichel referred to narcissistic supply being obtained from the environment, I regard the fuel that I draw as being even more specific in terms of where I get it. I obtain it from the emotional response of those around me. The quality of the fuel varies dependent on the type of emotional response and the proximity of the supplier. I will go into greater detail about that in a chapter below. You will be very interested to learn just how we grade the fuel that seek and later receive.

Any kind of emotional response serves to provide us with fuel. From happiness to adoration and from anger to upset through to delight and frustration. There are some who refer to my kind and me as emotional vampires. The description is entirely appropriate. We feed off your emotional responses and therefore it is imperative that we always create an emotional response from you. The greater the intensity of that response is, then the more intense fuel we receive. Even knowing that you will react in an emotional fashion, even though we may not see it, provides us with fuel. We suck it up every where we can.

We regard all emotional energy as sustenance. A lack of emotion causes us concern and will result (eventually) in our detachment and our seeking the same from an alternative source. There are those that suggest that we derive fuel from certain inanimate objects, for instance, status symbols. The expensive vehicle, tailor-made suit and the large house all apparently provide us with fuel. It is true that we covet these things as they accord with our sense of entitlement. They also enable us to demonstrate to the wider world our success and achievement. We crave such materialistic representation of success. However, we do not desire the Rolex watch, Ipad Mac or diamond-encrusted mobile telephone in themselves. We want those items because of the responses that they create in others. Those who see us drive by in a Bentley convertible invariably stand and stare open-mouthed. That reaction to our prestige provides us with fuel. The admiring glances that we draw when we walk through the department at work in an excellent suit provide us with fuel.

The compliments we receive for the style of shoes, holiday cottage we own and the extravagant party we have laid on are all fuel to us. Inanimate objects are the platforms for the provision of our fuel. Whilst some marvel at our choice of motor vehicle others will express jealousy and envy. Those reactions provide us with fuel as well. The cutting comment that accompanies a green-eyed stare is lost on us. The words evaporate, as it is the emotion that is bundled up inside those words and the stare that we want. You have noticed us and you have reacted to our presence. As Oscar Wilde put it so well,

"There is only one thing in life worse than being talked about, and that is not being talked about."

Our fascination and reliance on the inanimate object and the part that it plays in the provision of fuel does not end with what you may regard as traditional inanimate objects. The most effective inanimate object that we engage with is a person. You. How can we regard a person as an inanimate object? In the same way that the words in a scathing comment dissipate as we seize on the emotion, the identity of those providing us with fuel slips to one side as we savour the fuel that we can extract. Those of you who we seduce and draw into our world where we can draw deep on your fuel stand to be regarded as nothing more than an appliance. We see no person. We recognise no identity. What we see in a machine that has one purpose and one purpose alone. The provision of fuel for us. You have been selected because we know that you will provide us with the sweetest and most potent fuel. You have been chosen for your reliability and the volume at which you churn it out. We press your buttons and you deliver. That is the simple equation by which we engage you. You are no different to a washing machine, blue-ray player or dishwasher. We tap in what is required and you supply it to us. The provision of fuel goes beyond any sense of who you are. Your characteristics are subsumed.

We see you become part of us. Like the blood that pumps around our body, you are the fuel that keeps us alive. You are an integral part of our existence. We no longer see you as a separate and distinct person, but instead you become part of our system. You might liken it to a remote controlled car. The car has no power unless it is fitted with some batteries. Once those batteries have been added then the car can run. The movement of the car drains the batteries and they must be recharged or replaced. In the same way, we regard you as being slotted into us since you are a fuel cell. You are there to provide us with power. The emotional energy that you create provides us with the fuel that powers us. Once that energy starts to wane we must recharge it. We must find different ways of causing you to emit this emotional energy. If you fail to do so, then you will be put to one side (although never entirely forgotten about - more on that later) and replaced with something more potent.

Our fuel is emotional reaction. It is provided by everybody that we interact with but it is always at its sweetest and most potent when it is drawn from those nearest to us. Someone like you.

How Do We Obtain Fuel?

The carefully constructed image that we show to you and the world is designed to do two things. The first is to harvest fuel. The second is (with the necessary assistance of the fuel) to keep the dark creature that lurks inside of us hidden away. I will discuss this is in greater detail when I write about why we need the fuel. Let us begin by addressing the first point. By showing the world how magnificent and brilliant we are, how charming and affectionate we are and how interesting and entertaining we are, we expect the world to recognise this and provide us with our fuel.

This is why when we first encounter you, you see only a charming, delightful and attentive person. We only show this positive side of ourselves; the illusion that we have created, because if we allowed the creature to be seen you would not engage with us and therefore you would not provide us with any fuel. We appear as if angelic, riding into town on a unicorn that gallops over a rainbow. We radiate delight, excitement and success. We take such an interest in you, exhibit apparent care for you and your person and seem to be the person that dreams are made of.

All of this carefully constructed illusion is designed to make you give us fuel. If a narcissist has ensnared you, think back to the beginning and how we seduced you as we embarked on that golden period. Consider how those first few weeks panned out. I will describe below the process, which will be similar to your own and in bold I will describe how each step the narcissist took that step provided him or her with fuel.

The initial interaction will have been out of the blue. We might have been a supposed stranger in a bar (although we knew all about you beforehand), a longstanding acquaintance, someone from your teenage years or a colleague.

Our approach will have been unexpected yet welcomed as we arrived with a declaration of interest in you that was long-standing but never before mentioned.

(Your surprise, delight and interest)

Repeated compliments are paid, we listen to you attentively and ask lots of questions about you.

(Your delight in being made the centre of attention is palpable, you react warmly to our compliments thanking us for them and you praise us for our attentiveness)

We talk about our success, we are recognised by others and warmly greeted, and we demonstrate job security and progress, material trappings of success.

(You show obvious pleasure in being sat with a popular person, you praise us for our success, you ask us about what we have achieved, giving us attention by doing so)

We contact you repeatedly by telephone, text message and in person.

(You always answer the phone and message us straight back underlining how important we are to you; you are always pleased to see us.)

We give you gifts and take you to exciting and lavish places.

(You thank us for our generosity and express delight with it, you marvel at our largesse)

We repeatedly touch you, hold you and kiss you.

(You respond in a similar fashion providing us with this tactile attention, whilst praising us for our intimate nature)

We spend a lot of time with you.

(You welcome us doing so reflecting how important we are to you.)

We introduce you into our social circle.

(You reciprocate and your friends remark how wonderful we are in our treatment of you.)

We explain our future plans to you, which will now involve you.

(You express your delight and satisfaction at this, you explain how marvellous we are and how fortunate you feel to have us in your life.)

We compliment you excessively, even when it is not merited.

(You feel pleased and show your delight towards us, you feel obligated to compliment us in return.)

We carry out tasks and chores for you.

(You always thank us and remark how wonderful we are for doing these things. You think of ways you can return the favour and thus make us the centre of your attention.)

Everything described there is regarded as a positive action on our part. Nearly everyone (save those who would heed the red flags) would welcome being treated in this manner. Nearly everyone would respond in the way that I have described. You can see how all of the things that my kind have said and done are nothing to do with being interested in you. The gifts, the compliments and the support are all executed in order to provoke a positive reaction from you.

In the same way that I drive up and down in a gleaming new top-of-the-range Mercedes Benz so that people point and give me admiring glances, all of these things are done to elicit a positive response from you. We expect if of you. It is something we do with everyone. Whether they are a lover, family member, friend or colleague. We show this wonderful illusion so we are admired and liked by everyone who comes into contact with it. Who could fail not to respond in this way? The result is fuel.

If this fuel is not provided voluntarily then we will demand it and force it from those around us. We recognise no boundaries so we will proceed as we see fit in order to gather this fuel. It is possible for us to gather positive fuel (for instance we ask what you think of our new shoes and you declare that you like them even though you would not have commented if we had not drawn your attention to them) through forcing a response from you but more often than not where we must extort it, the reaction is often negative in nature. It may surprise you to find that we find negative fuel more edifying and invigorating than positive fuel. The reason for this is that people always want others to be pleasant to them and therefore the positive reaction that being pleasant generates is not really all that difficult to achieve and is given readily. The reaction that arises from behaviour that is designed to create a negative response is not always forthcoming. Most normal people will try and keep their anger under control, hide their upset, manage their frustration and so on. As a normal person they will try and resolve the situation through discussion and suggestion, preferring to pay attention to the behaviour of the other person (namely us) in deciding how best to respond. They are an empathic person and therefore they are focussed on others, not themselves. It is only after sustained behaviour that their negative emotional response can be extracted. After a period of savage name-calling it is only then that they begin to cry (of course over time the emotional reaction comes sooner and sooner and that is why we must increase its intensity each time and derive it from different sources as there is the law of diminishing returns to take into account). It will take sustained provocation to cause you to lose your temper eventually. However, the pay-off is that the intensity of these emotional responses is such that the fuel they generate is immense and that is why we regard negative emotional responses over positive ones. You will regard this as unpleasant and a horrendous way for a person to have to go through life. It is a fact. It is the way that we obtain our fuel and that means generating an emotional response from those around us.

It will be instructive at this point to compare and contrast a typical day for you and a typical one for us in order to see how our behaviour is geared towards obtaining fuel. This is premised on you and I residing together in an established relationship and the golden period has long since gone. I will insert **(PF)** for positive fuel or **(NF)** for negative fuel, after each instance where fuel is generated for either you, in the first example, or for me, in the second example.

You wake up and cuddle me, as I lie sleeping. You run your fingers through my hair and then rise. You go and prepare breakfast and you make breakfast for me. You greet me when I come downstairs for breakfast and ask if I slept well. I sit and read the morning paper as you attend to me providing breakfast and asking what I have planned at work. You ask me to collect some dry cleaning but I refuse explaining I have an engagement after work. I do not tell you what this engagement is and my refusal irks you slightly. You agree to collect the dry cleaning. I leave you to clear away the breakfast dishes as I return upstairs and ready myself for work.

I leave for work kissing you on the cheek **(PF)** as I leave. You wish me a good day and wave to me as I back the car out of the drive. You select the meat for the evening meal and leave it to defrost before getting ready for work. You tidy the bathroom up after me and shake your head because I have left a damp towel on the bed again. On your side.

You leave for work and on arrival one of your colleagues compliments you on the fragrance that you are wearing **(PF)**. You attend to your job in an office and in your morning post receive a thank you card from a grateful client **(PF)**. You work on a project all morning and send me a couple of text messages asking how I am and asking what wine I would like to accompany the evening meal. I do not reply. A friend who was going to the nearby coffee shop hands you a coffee and she has remembered your favourite type of coffee **(PF)**. You meet a friend for lunch. She is having some trouble at home and you listen and offer constructive advice. Your lunch is interrupted by three telephone calls from me. You do not answer, as you do not wish to interrupt your friend. She thanks you for supporting her **(PF)** before leaving. You call me back and I demonstrate my annoyance at you not answering the 'phone when I had called. You apologise and attempt to speak to me about the evening meal but I put the 'phone down.

You ring me twice but I do not answer. You send three text messages repeating your apology and asking what I want for dessert. I do not answer.

You return to work and your boss thanks you for delivering a report last week, which he found very helpful **(PF)**. He asks you to join him for a drink after work by way of thanks, but you decline explaining you already have plans. You continue with your work and take a call from another friend and discuss arrangements for going out at the weekend. You call me again but the call goes straight to voicemail. You return home and prepare the evening meal. You call me twice trying to ascertain when I will be home but I do not answer. You continue with the meal preparation and keep it warm as you wait for me to return.

I arrive just before 9pm. You politely ask where I have been and explain you had been trying to contact me to discuss when dinner was required. I react to your query with irritation and then anger and provoke an argument. You are tired and become upset. I leave you with the food and head to the study. After a time, you gather yourself and come to speak to me in a gesture of conciliation. I do not reciprocate and a further argument ensues at my creation. You leave the study and return downstairs.

You eat and watch television before clearing everything away and ironing my shirt for the following day. You head up to bed and lie waiting for me to join you. You hear the door to the spare room close and realise I have chosen to sleep in there. You turn on to your side and fighting back tears attempt to sleep.

You will see that there were six instances of fuel gathered by you in this example. You did not seek any of those instances and I provided only one of them to you. Now, contrast this with how I go about my day. I have chosen a fairly standard day, rather than one where I am going hell for leather to acquire fuel. Nevertheless, I suggest that you buckle up.

You cuddle me **(PF)** as I pretend to sleep so I do not respond to your affection **(NF)**. I wait until you have gone downstairs and check my mobile 'phone. There are several messages from a potential target that I am engaged in a text message flirtation with **(PF)**. I send her a reply and there is an instant response **(PF)**. I go downstairs and you greet me asking if I slept well **(PF)**. I complain that the pillows you have recently bought are too soft and you agree to get me some harder ones **(PF)**. You ask me what I have planned at work **(PF)**. You ask me to get some dry cleaning after work but I refuse and explain I have an existing engagement **(PF)**. I can see my refusal has irked you along with my refusal to explain what my engagement is **(NF)**. You agree to collect the dry cleaning and attend to clearing away the dishes **(PF)**.

I return upstairs and check my phone to find another message from the prospect **(PF)**. I check my e-mails and find there is one thanking me for a deal I have closed **(PF)** a further one which shows my billing to be the highest for the year to date **(PF)** and I append this chart to an e-mail to a competitor with a suitable bragging post **(NF)**. I get dressed and admire my appearance in the mirror. I take a picture and sent it to the prospect that immediately responds with a complimentary comment **(PF)**.

(I am not even out of the house yet and have already harvested fifteen different instances of fuel)

I have left the bathroom a mess and I have deliberately placed a damp towel on the bed as I know this irritates you **(NF)**. I head downstairs and kiss you good-bye, although I opt to kiss you on the cheek rather than the mouth because I can choose to do this **(PF) (No negative fuel as you did not react to negatively to me choosing your cheek instead)**. I get in my car and call a friend to organise a drink later in the week. I spend the first ten minutes of the conversation declaring how well I am doing at work and he responds with compliments to this **(PF)**. I repeatedly block his attempts to tell me his news. His frustration shows in his response. **(NF)**. As I pull up at some traffic lights I notice the young driver next to me admiring my car and he gives me a thumbs up **(PF)**. I overtake several cars on my way to the office **(PF)** and cut one driver up. I see him angrily gesticulate at me from his less expensive car and I laugh in response **(NF)**

On arrival at the office my secretary has a cup of tea waiting for me **(PF)**. During the day I secure a new deal which draws praise from my boss **(PF)**, spread a few lies about a competitor and later overhear him complaining about them although he has no idea where they have come from **(NF)**. A secretary I have not seen before smiles at me **(PF)**. I stop by and chat to her for a while and she is clearly flirting with me **(PF)**. I dress down a junior employee on a flimsy basis and he looks crestfallen **(NF)**. I receive two text messages from you about dinner but I ignore them which I know will make you feel dejected **(NF)** and I continue with a few flirtatious texts with the new prospect **(PF)**. I land a load of work on a junior employee's desk. She starts to complain but I put her in her place **(NF)**. I attend the gym at lunchtime and am met with several admiring glances from male and female attendees as I work out **(PF)**. I return to the office and remark how out of shape a colleague is looking which leaves him fuming since I walk away before he is able to respond with his own explanation **(NF)**. I telephone you three times and you do not answer so I leave you a nasty voicemail **(NF)**. You ring me back and I have a go at you as you try to apologise **(NF)** and then I hang up on you **(NF)**. You call me twice but I ignore the calls **(NF)** and I also ignore your text messages **(NF)**.

I circulate a congratulatory e-mail I have received from a client and receive several responses acknowledging my achievement **(PF)**. I secure petty cash to pay for my drinks this evening even though it has nothing to do with work and the look my secretary gives me as she hands me the cash confirms she knows this to be the case but she knows better than to complain **(PF)**. You telephone me and I cut your call off straight away **(NF)**.

I go to a bar straight from work and whilst I am waiting for a female friend I chat-up the bargirl. She is responsive to my overtures and gives me her number **(PF)**. I sit and flirt with my female friend **(PF)** and spend my time explaining how hard my home life is despite all the things that I do because of the way you treat me. She laps it up and is most sympathetic **(PF)**. She asks to meet me next week and I agree. **(PF)**. You call me twice but I deliberately do not answer. **(NF)**. I catch a taxi home and on the way tell a junior employee to head back to work to deliver my car to my house even though he is busy with his family **(NF)**. I accuse the taxi driver of taking the wrong route. He argues back so I don't give him the full fare and take his licence details. **(NF)**. I enter the house and you politely ask where I have been. I regard this as an unnecessary attack so I provoke an argument **(NF)**. I ensconce myself in the study where I engage in some online flirtation **(PF)**. You come to see me to smooth matters over but I provoke another argument, which makes you cry **(NF)**. I continue with my online antics and sign up to a dating site to punish you for arguing with me **(PF)**. I hear you head for bed and I decide to watch some pornographic videos turning the volume up in the hope you will hear **(NF)** before I noisily head to the spare room so you know that I have decided to sleep in there rather than with you. **(NF)**

There we are. You should have counted fifty-four different instances of fuel, of different types, some positive and some negative and from different sources. Truth be told, I was not even trying too hard to harvest all of that either. That is representative of a typical day and you will see from that how often and how repeated it was necessary for me to gather fuel. In many instances, it was as it should be. The fuel was offered up as a matter of course through people doing things for me and admiring me. In some instances, I had to extract it by engaging in flirtation, seeking praise or denigrating others. You will notice how it runs all the way through my day. It is not a case of being able to top-up (that is impossible) at the start of the day and cruise through it on one injection of fuel. There has to be repeated supplies throughout the day. You will observe as well how much of it was based on how people responded to me but also how I imagined them to be responding to some of the things that I do or do not do. Knowing how you will react, because I have conditioned you that way, will result in the provision of fuel for me as well.

Where I face criticism (when you question me where I have been) I react by provoking an argument. This not only is done to obtain fuel but to enable me to maintain my superiority in the face of unnecessary questioning from someone who does not have the standing to do so. All through my day I have to obtain fuel and this is an example of how it is done. You can see how vastly different it is to the normal actions of you.

There are thousands of ways of obtaining fuel (thankfully) and we are the masters at knowing how to do it. Naturally, the frequency by which we can harvest fuel from people varies and therefore we need wide-ranging dramatis personae. You will also note that I obtained fuel from nearly everybody who I interacted with, no matter how brief or inconsequential. Engaging with someone and not doing extracting some form of fuel is a wasted opportunity and I am always planning and plotting the ways I can acquire fuel. Each time there has to be a reaction, either positive or negative. As time passes in our relationship I will generally obtain almost exclusively negative fuel from you (aside from when I deign to give you a glimpse of the golden period) as even when you are trying to be pleasant to me and do things for me, I will regard them as an irritation and provoke anger, tears, upset and so on. These negative emotions provide me with a greater level of fuel. I need to obtain that from you for two fundamental reasons.

1.   Familiarity breeds contempt. The longer I am with you, the less potent your positive fuel becomes because I have been repeatedly exposed to it. Thus I have to shift to the more promising negative fuel with the unpleasant consequence this has for you; and

2.   Over time you may start to see through my construct and therefore I have to work harder to keep it in place. I deal more with the construct in a later chapter. In order to maintain the illusion of my magnificence and brilliance, I must lash out at you to gather the fuel to maintain my power and control.

Thus, this is how I acquire fuel. It will be similar for my brethren and we always follow the same pattern.

1.   Seduction at first to gather positive fuel and make the fall during devaluation that much steeper thus generating more potent fuel;

2.   Devaluation to produce negative fuel. The worsening of my behaviour being designed to make the third element more potent;

3.   Occasional return to the golden period in order to garner more positive fuel and then lift you up in readiness to cast you down once more;

4.   Discarding you but only then to allow me to Hoover you back in which provides extremely potent fuel when it works.

5.   Having secured your return the devaluation commences again.

All of this push and pull behaviour and this whole merry-go-round is designed to provide me with fuel from the emotional reactions that you give. It also allows my kind and me to contrast the emotions, thus producing a better quality of fuel. This is how we obtain our fuel.

What Do We Want?

What does the narcissist want? What do I want? What do members of my brethren want, be they male, female or transgender, a father, a mother, a sibling, a lover, a boss or a neighbour? We want one thing and one thing only. Fuel. Not only do we want fuel, we need it. It is the first thing we think of when we wake and it is the last thing that goes through our minds as we drift into slumber. Fuel defines us. Fuel drives us. Fuel is everything. We must gather it often and repeatedly and we seek it from a multiplicity of sources. The ways we obtain it are wide-ranging and fascinating in their ingenuity and horrifying in their brutality. The fuel can be divided into two categories. Positive fuel, which provides us with an ego boost, and negative fuel, which arises from hurting others.

Each and every day we do so by making you love us, admire us and adore us. By praising our brilliance, marvelling at our superiority and hailing our god-like magnificence. By craving us and worshipping us. By shining your spotlights on us. By seeking your sympathy. By playing the victim. By lying. By lying. By lying again. By issuing excuses. By using you, exploiting you and draining you. By taking your money and your possessions. By isolating you and scaring you. By having you run around for us, jump for us and pander to us. By comparing you to others, by making you anxious and by making you walk on eggshells. By promising the world, jam tomorrow and showing you heaven. By changing the rules that never applied in the first place. By raising the bar and moving the goal posts. By putting you down, mocking you and insulting you. By making you take the blame and by making you feel guilty. By making you scream, cry and sob. By wounding you and hurting you. By confusing and bewildering you. By pushing you and pulling you and pushing you and pulling you. By lifting you up and casting you down. By binding you to us and by sucking you into our world. By false promises and empty apologies. By existing.

Fuel means everything to us. Everybody around us is a source of fuel. We regard each person that comes within our sphere of influence as an appliance. Your sole purpose is to dispense delicious fuel for us. Those who we ensnare in an intimate relationship provide the most potent and delicious fuel, which makes us feel powerful and omnipotent. This fuel causes us to feel like the gods that we know we are. We are entitled to this fuel. It is ours by right and nothing must ever get in our way in our ceaseless quest for it. We can never get enough fuel. There is always room for more. There is always the opportunity for another compliment to massage our egos or for a scathing comment to be directed your way to assert our superiority over you. Our fuel tank never shows as full, it cannot overflow because it just becomes larger and larger to accommodate the growing need for fuel.

Why do we need it? We need it to keep the beast under control. The craven creature that lurks waiting to wound and injure us can only be kept within its prison through the obtaining of fuel. This creature is always waiting to escape and wreak havoc by trying to remind us of what we are, of our failings and our weaknesses. I do not wish to give this creature much attention for even as I type this paragraph the sense of anguish rises at the recollection of this creature. But it is its existence, which drives our quest for fuel. I know I will have to deal with this creature in terms of giving you additional insight so I shall save it until later.

Let me provide you with an insight as to how, at this moment in time, I have organised my world to ensure that I have several appliances supplying me with fuel so that I can have a degree of comfort that there is fuel available and I am not suddenly going to run dry.

I have a girlfriend called Kim. I do not live with her but she spends most of her time at my homes. We have been seeing one another for a number of months. I still find her interesting and thus she has not been subjected to the devaluation yet. Maybe she is the one who can provide me with the salvation that I seek? For now, however she lavishes her praise and appreciation on me as a consequence of the admission I have granted her into my carefully fabricated heaven. She is clearly enjoying her stay. (In case you are wondering, she cannot learn of this or any of my publications so the reality of what I am remains unknown to her (and others I may add)).

Kim is an intelligent and elegant lady. She takes an interest in the news, reads a quality newspaper, enjoys reading books and has a particular interest in the legacies of European powers in their former colonies. She is knowledgeable and stimulating but she regularly seeks my opinion on a variety of topics and thus this reinforces my importance and superiority. Her attention to her appearance is as a consequence of her wanting to look her best for me and the reaction she draws from those who see her, both male and female, gives me a sense of pride that she is on my arm. It also bolsters my innate superiority because she is with me and she is not with them. She organises dinner parties at my city home because she regards the view from the dining room as better than the one from hers. This is something that her friends concur with when they visit and only goes to increase my satisfaction at having such a view readily available. It is evident they do not. Kim and I speak frequently and we are not at the stage where I have to bombard her with text messages and telephone calls but rather she has been conditioned to call me first thing in the morning (when we are not together) and so begins the daily diet of repeated communications. I do not recall the last time I called her. It is very much one way now and that is a position I like to attain. Kim provides me with a strong supply of positive fuel from her admiration and adoration of me. Let's see how long that will last for shall we?

I am currently engaged in a fairly low level flirtation with a lady named Samantha. I occasionally meet her for a drink and our texts ping backwards and forwards frequently. I have managed to position her so that if she does not hear from me for a while, she will keep messaging me. Her messages are never questioning or haranguing but rather praising me as she seeks to elicit from me one of my charming observations about her that has her melt inside. She seems to have learned that there is nothing to be gained from pressing me and I am content with that state of affairs. The collection of messages that she sends me provides me with occasional delightful dollops of fuel throughout my day. I will reel her in as I see fit at the appropriate time. Should Kim let me down (and I have every expectation that she will because I have always been let down in the past) then Samantha will replace her as the object of my affections in the hope that she can deliver where others have failed to do so in the past. For now, she remains a good supplier of fuel. She is reliable and best of all undemanding. Accordingly, I do not have to apply much effort in order to receive fuel from her.

On the other side of the coin is Andrea. She let me down and then had the temerity to try and distance herself from me. I am currently engaged in a campaign to let her know that she cannot do that. I make the decisions and she has to abide by them. She disgusts and irritates me with her whining voice and scrawny arms. I am using several false e-mail accounts to bombard her with e-mails throughout the course of the day and night. She has changed her personal account twice already but she is unaware that I have a Lieutenant in her camp that keeps me apprised of changes to her e-mail address and her mobile telephone number. I have a couple of my admirers engaged in sending her hateful and personal e-mails, largely revolving around her eating disorder which has clearly reared its head again. I did help her with this when we were in a relationship.

I ensured she ate properly and frequently so that she became a healthy and attractive weight. I barred her way to the bathroom after a meal when she sought to induce vomiting. I kept her close to me as I showed her how she could be looked after. Of course she failed me and my anger at her failure to provide me with the levels of fuel that I demand and need meant I subjected her to a vicious period of devaluation and demeaning denigration. She clung on and then received some help from her auntie who was concerned not only about her plummeting weight but also her state of mind and thus she sought to escape me, aided by auntie. She disgusts me now and I question what it is that I ever saw in her. I scold myself for having been so weak as to think that I could help her. She is beyond help. She would rather be selfish and make herself thin and ill so it is all about her rather than continue to give me what I need. I helped her over and over again and she repays me by trying to escape me. Well, she has no chance. This e-mail campaign will not let up as she is reminded of what a horrible person she is and how we all know this. I have no interest in having her back, she is too weak a person to be associated with someone as powerful as me, but my helpers show me the occasional responses she has penned by way of response. She really ought to ignore them if she knew what was good for her, but she thinks she is cleverer than me and always wants the last word. Well, it is of no use to her as all it does is provides me with some fuel resulting from her hysterical responses that she types and the fact I know that I loom large inside her mind.

I have two sources of fuel at work in the form of Eric and Angela. Both of them are junior to me and keen to obtain a promotion. There is of course only one promotion available and it is a fight to the death between these two. The elevation in status of course is in my gift and they both know this. This results in them looking to curry favour with me on a repeated basis and thus this provides me with intermittent fuel from their earnest brown-nosing behaviour in the workplace.

Added to this is Tom who I suppose one would call him a best friend although I prefer to describe him as the best provider of non-intimate fuel. Tom adores me and if it were not for the fact that he is married and has two children, I would say he has a crush on me. I have known him a long time and I have been content to keep him around me. From time to time he annoys me and therefore he has to be put down and reminded of his place. It is only right. There are periods when I must subject him to a period of silent treatment which he understands is a clear reason for something he has done wrong. Tom is ever loyal and always looking for ways to please me. That is why I keep him around and he has his uses.

He will always do as I ask, never flinching from the task. If I tell him that Kim is the most wonderful person in the world, he will agree and reel off the reasons why that is the case. If the next day I were to tell him that I hate Kim and she is a bitch her will agree and find twenty reasons to support my position without ever questioning this sudden shift in my affections. He knows better than most how people repeatedly let me down and therefore they must be punished for their transgressions. I see no need to ever crush Tom because although he does let me down he will rebound like a Labrador puppy fuelled by an energy drink and come bounding up eager to please me notwithstanding the vicious and scathing humiliations I have subjected him to. He is a loyal servant and provides me with both positive and negative fuel. Since he is not going anywhere he is spared obliteration.

Accordingly, I have matters structured as follows: -

1. Kim. Intimate relationship and supplier of potent positive fuel.

2. Samantha. Flirtation. Supplier of positive fuel. Contingency for when Kim falls from grace.

3. Andrea. Source of negative fuel. She who must be destroyed.

4. Eric and Angela. Sources of positive workplace fuel.

5. Tom. Source of positive and negative fuel. Mr Reliable. A true appliance.

Now add to that the sprinkling of fuel from the minions that I am prone to putting down from time to time (the waiters, the car park attendants, the officer juniors and so on), the dusting of admiring glances that I draw when I am out and about, the pinch of fuel from those who wish to do business with me and therefore sing my praises and the occasional spurt of fuel as I reach out a tendril to Hoover back in a victim from the past and you can see that I have many and varied ways of acquiring the ever so precious fuel.

It isn't easy maintaining all these networks and I do think back to when I was younger and the approach was somewhat more chaotic. Back then I would have in place a relationship but I found them tedious and soon lost interest in the other person so I would be engaged in putting them down because they had let me down. I occupied my time sweeping bars for new sources of fuel in order to try to keep the craving at bay. It was often laborious as I identified new prospects and sought to reel them in. I soon polished my craft however and as my prestige and standing increased I found that my seduction became easier and easier and the victim's need to cling on to me became more intense.

I was quite the catch. The prize that they did not wish to lose. I ensured I obtained my fuel but it was in a more haphazard fashion and as a consequence I found that I would at times be vacillating between the positive and negative fuel much more violently and gathering it from a whole array of sources with often little regard to the quality of the fuel that I was receiving. I have learned from those early forays into the acquisition of fuel and have sought to create an infrastructure that suits my needs more readily. Nevertheless, no matter how structured this is and how much planning I apply to this task the pursuit of fuel will never go away. There is always some more to be gathered be it from an admiring glance or lashing out at those who always manage to offend me.

You will find it difficult to comprehend how the necessity of obtaining this fuel preoccupies us. It is like a nagging itch that no matter how often one scratches it just will not go away. You see the world in a different fashion to us and you obtain your fuel from helping people, caring and looking after them. You have been created and wired in a different way to us. I do not know if the gathering of your fuel has you obsessed in the way that we are. I do not care either.

All I know that is I must always be looking for new ways to gain this fuel, ways of wringing more from existing sources, channels of fuel from those who might have thought they have escaped me, supply lines laid down for future fuel to flow my way. It is a mammoth operation and invariably will involve many people as our appliances and this carries with it a need for more energy from my kind and me. Not something that we are keen to have to do but we must if we are to survive.

There is one way however that this process can be made much simpler. There is a method of gaining this fuel and doing so by much reducing the number of appliances that we are reliant on. This need for fuel will not go away. All that we can do is devise new methods of obtaining it and look to do so in more efficient and effective ways. The holy grail of the supply of fuel is to acquire someone who is co-dependent. This is akin to striking a huge oil supply in the desert, uncovering a massive seam of gold underground or a scientist discovering a new form of energy.

We must have fuel. To have it come almost exclusively from one source is something we desire most highly. It reduces the need to find other sources. It removes the uncertainty that arises with other sources that they may dry up or become less potent and thus force us to take action (and use up energy) in order to ensure we obtain our fuel. The co-dependent provides this for us. That is why they are highly prized. We want fuel but if we managed to ensnare a co-dependent then we have hit the jackpot.

What Are The Sources of Fuel?

We have established that my kind and me exist for one thing and for one thing only, fuel. I have in the examples given above of a typical day and also of how I have structured my current networks given you some insight into how I gather my fuel. However, what about the narcissist you are involved in? How does he or she gather his or fuel? How do they regard the various sources involved? Who should you be considering would be used as sources other than you? These might involve people competing with you and it is likely you will be triangulated with them, so it is certainly worth your while trying to establish who they might be.

How do we regard the various ways the fuel is provided to us? In the examples above I have given many instances of how this fuel is gathered, but what fuel do we regard as the weakest and which is the most potent? Knowing this will give you a distinct advantage in dealing with the narcissist in your life. By knowing what makes him or her tick, you can take the appropriate action.

You may find it rather interesting that fuel does not feel the same irrespective of who provides and the method of delivery. On the contrary, the person who supplies it and how it is supplied are extremely important and this plays a huge factor in our behaviour. By letting you know who provides the best fuel and in what method, you are gaining a keen insight into what to look for, what to avoid and know what is likely to happen when your narcissist feels that he or she is running low on fuel. I mention in a chapter below what happens when fuel supplies happen to run low.

The nature of fuel is that it is afforded a grading. Naturally, we want the best fuel, as often as possible and from the fewest number of sources. That is why we love to ensnare an empathic individual and ensure that they remain close at hand. Even better is a co-dependent. The co-dependent represents the platinum standard of supply and I provide you with my observations on this in greater detail in **Chained: The Narcissist's Co-Dependent**. I have touched on this categorising that I detail below, in **Chained** but it is worth repeating here, as it is most relevant to the topic.

Who provides us with the most potent, the most delicious and the most powerful fuel? Again, this requirement is drawn from our need to be efficient in our energy expenditure. Since we are creatures that are entitled to anything and everything, we see no reason why we must apply ourselves to an exhausting degree to secure our aims. This applies most of all to the acquisition of fuel. It makes perfect sense.

If we drain ourselves in searching for the fuel, when we obtain it we will need more again to imbue us with the power, impregnability and superiority that come from it. Either that or we reconcile ourselves to our hit only providing us with a much smaller degree of power and a shorter period of omnipotence. We cannot reconcile ourselves to doing this because this means we have less power to keep the craven creature in check. Accordingly, we need to be efficient and effective in securing our fuel. We want lots of it, preferably from almost one source and of the sweetest and most invigorating type. How do we determine who provides us with the best fuel? There is logic to this.

You may not regard my kind and me as the type of people who are logical. In fact, our very behaviour seems to be born out of chaos since everywhere we go we leave behind an aftermath of destruction. When it comes to gathering fuel we are methodical. We have a strategy in place which we update on a daily basis. We assess and monitor in order to ensure we secure the best fuel, in the fastest way possible and from the most reliable source. We are disciplined in how we approach this exercise. We have to be because we do not want to contemplate what might happen if we do not apply ourselves in an effective fashion to the harvesting of fuel. We set our sights on the potential appliances and calculate how these will be brought into our spheres of influence. We work out how we can best secure these supplies of fuel. We ascertain how often they will supply us and how long they are likely to last. All of this is being calculated by us. Ever wondered why we never have much time for you? Now you know. We are too busy plotting and scheming how our fuel harvesting campaign will proceed. If we actually sat down and wrote in a notebook our thoughts for gathering fuel I daresay you would be taken aback at how organised it its, how effective and how clinical it is. We are an instrument designed to harvest fuel.

The qualitative effect of the fuel that we seek is dependent on two factors. The proximity of the source and the form of delivery. First of all, I shall detail for you the proximity of the source commencing with the weakest and rising to the strongest. There are increasing degrees of the quality of the fuel dependent on which type of appliance is providing us with the fuel. This is something we have to factor into our deliberations when we are deciding whether we should expend energy on a target and if we decide that we should, and then we need to consider just how much should be expended. Naturally, we are not going to apply a lot of energy when we are dealing with the weakest types of proximity of source. Instead we will look to allow those providers occur just to chance rather than seek them out and expend energy on them. Conversely, we will consider using larger amounts of energy when it comes to those higher up the proximity scale. Let's looks at this scale and then I will elaborate a little on the various categories. They are ranked in ascending order, weakest first.

Proximity of the Source

Remote strangers

Strangers

Minions

Acquaintances

Colleagues

Outer Circle Friends

Inner Circle Friends

Family

Intimate Partners

Former Intimate Partners (devalue "DV"))

Former Intimate Partners (hoover("H"))

What does each of these categories mean?

Remote strangers contain people who we do not know and we are not actually physically near to. A classic example would be someone who we do not know on Facebook sending a friend request. The fact that there has been some interaction by them providing us with attention, even in such a small dose does provide us with fuel. You would not react to this and you probably would not respond to the request. We do. We gain fuel from it and we immediately engage as we sense more fuel can be gathered from this newly acquired "friend". This may explain part of the fascination with social media that your narcissist has. Along with the other interactions that occur on it, the existence of Facebook forms a background provision of fuel. The remotes strangers are people we do not know and who we are not in the same physical space as. Invariably our interaction will be through electronic means.

Strangers are people we do not know but who we are close to in the physical sense. For instance, they might be somebody else walking along the pavement towards us or in a crowd at a concert or stood next to us in a bar. There is always scope for these people to interact with us in both a positive and negative fashion.

Minions are those people that we do not know but are tasked with doing something for us by reason of being a service provider in some way. This includes taxi drivers, waiters, bank clerks, delivery drivers, ticket collectors, call centre operatives and so on. These people are unlikely to be known to us but they rank above strangers because they have an obligation towards us. They are obliged to answer our query, or lodge our deposit or serve us a meal. That obligation means they are inferior to us from the beginning and thus means their interaction has the potential to yield more fuel than that from a stranger. I should imagine you would find such a distinction odd, indeed when I have explained this to people previously I am met with a mixture of puzzled looks and amazement. Whatever your reaction may be, this distinction and the effect that arises from it, is real.

Acquaintances are people who know us but effectively only by sight or name. They may happen to have an obligation towards us, for example, the barman who we see twice a week knows our name and remembers us, but knows no more than that. What matters most is the fact that they know who we are. We do not care if we recall who they are, they are inconsequential save for their capacity to provide us with fuel. Since they know us, they are interested in us and this increases the potency of their fuel.

The category of Colleagues is next. They know us, interact with us and invariably will also have an obligation to us. They will know more about us by reason of their frequent interaction with us and this means that they will have a greater appreciation of our abilities, meaning their fuel becomes of a higher grade than those who rank below them on the list.

Outer Circle Friends. These people know more about our lives than colleagues. They have an obligation to us by reason of social interaction. We see them with reasonable frequency although the members of this class can change often also. The degree of interaction that they have with us, combined with their knowledge and appreciation of us, increases their potential fuel yield.

Inner Circle Friends. This group are longer-term friends who also see us more often and have often divulged more information to us about them. They have in all likelihood been brainwashed by our manipulation of them and therefore they have been programmed to remain with us and their default setting will be one of admiration.

Family are the next ranking. They are invariably long-standing in nature, interact with us frequently and know much about us. They have an emotional obligation towards us, which often proves their undoing, resulting in blind loyalty when they ought to know better.

Intimate Partners. The people we have relationships with, marry, possibly have children together and share a home. They know us in detail (or at least they know part of us in detail), interact with us on a daily basis and invest much of their lives in us through the ties that bind.

Former Intimate Partners (devalued). These are the cast-offs from our relationships that we have turned against. We are in the process of continuing a programme of devaluing of them even though we are no longer together.

Former Intimate Partners (hoover). These are the people we cast aside and denigrate who have then returned to us following a successful hoover. These people top the tree when it comes to the proximity of supply.

Take a moment to consider the narcissist you are involved with. Most likely if you are reading this you will be in one of the top four categories (maybe you belong to two at the same time if incest has reared its head. It is not unheard of). Next reflect on all the other people you know who have been swept up in the narcissist's chaos and carnage. Which categories do they belong to? Keep that in mind as how they are treated and engaged with is commensurate to their ranking.

It is not just the proximity of the source, which is a consideration when we are deciding where we will be obtaining the best type of fuel. The form of delivery must also be considered as well and in conjunction with the proximity of the source. I detail below the types of form of delivery, again commencing with the weakest first, followed by a brief explanation of each category to assist understanding

Form of Delivery

Awareness

Neutral Response

Acknowledgement

Loving Gesture

Loving Words

Attentive Gesture

Attentive Words

Admiring Gesture

Admiring Words

Angry Gesture

Angry Words

Tearful Gesture

Tearful Words

So, what do these categories mean?

Awareness means that we know that you will be thinking about us in some way. There will be nothing to tell us that you are actually doing this. Instead, it is based on us knowing the effects of our manipulative behaviour and how it is designed to cause you to think about us even when we are not around you. I explained in some detail in the book **Manipulated** the concept of ever presence. Ever presence can provoke different forms of delivery but the usual one is awareness. We know, from repeated application of these manipulative techniques that you will be thinking about us and this awareness of us creates a form of delivery of fuel.

Neutral response is where you communicate with us but do so in neither a good or bad way. When I refer to good or bad, I mean that a good reaction is one, which is admiring or loving in nature or something similar. Bad means anger or tears or such like. Naturally, a good or bad reaction is desirable and thus would be considered a good reaction, by us. A neutral response has some value albeit of a limited nature because you have interacted with us.

Acknowledgement is where you have recognised us and reacted to us but most importantly you have used my name. You may have only said "Hello H G" but the use of my name means you know me, you have accepted me and recognised the value in using my name. Again it is of use to me albeit at the lower end of the scale.

Loving Gesture. This category contains such things as a kiss or a hug. It may mean holdings hands or making love. You may be slightly surprised to see this as low as it is on this list. This is because we do not regard love as the most effective method of achieving the most potent fuel. Yes, it has a value but it is beneath other types of positive and negative methods. If this was a list appertaining to an empath's fuel then this would be near the top of the list, but in our world it ranks far lower.

The first reason is as stated; loving gestures are beneath other types. The second is that we actually do not like physical intimacy. It is used during the seduction phase because we know that you as an empath rate it very highly as a desirable part of a relationship. Being the chameleons that we are we will adjust to provide what you want in order to draw you into our world. This is with a view to receiving a better type of fuel from you in due course. We dislike the physical contact that you associate with these types of intimacy and the most cherished of those for you, making love, is regarded with horror by us as the relationship unfolds. We use these to draw you in and then to enable us to withdraw them later (in the hope it will prompt a response which is higher up the ladder of form of delivery) and we will use it again when we wish to Hoover you back in again.

Loving Words. This category is self-explanatory. You may have focussed on the fact that in this category (and those above it) that each time the category of words ranks higher than gestures. This is simply because we rely on words more than gestures (because they are much easier to use and also expend far less fuel) and consequently in respect of your form of delivery towards us, we place a greater value on words than we do on gestures. A further reason for this is that empathic individuals are very expressive, especially through the use of words. You like to write love letters, poetry and leave notes describing how you feel about us. You enjoy telling us what you feel for us and therefore because we know that words are important to you (as well as the fact they are important to us) they will then always rank higher than gestures in each particular category.

Attentive Gesture. This is doing something for us, whether it is cooking our evening meal, doing our laundry or buying us a new shirt. We like to have you running around after us as this underlines our importance and also plays to our sense of entitlement. If you are doing things for us, then this amounts to an attentive gesture. Note how we prefer you to make us a mug of tea to holding our hand. Would that apply to you? Never. That in itself gives you a huge insight into the way we are.

Attentive Words. This again equates to being prepared to do things for us and shows us that you are paying attention to us.

"How are you?"
"Are you warm enough?"
"Have you had plenty to eat?"
"You look tired; why don't you go have a nap?"

These are all examples of the normal and caring things that you will say to us. You are keeping your attention on us by having regard to our needs and welfare. This is only correct since we are entitled to this.

Admiring Gesture. Moving into the top half of this list we now start to get to those things, which really matter to us. See how admiration is ranked higher than love. Make a mental note of that fact. An admiring gesture will incorporate a look of appreciation, a wolf whistle and applause. It includes standing open mouthed and eyes wide, cheering and giving us the thumbs up. Would you really value a thumbs up over making love? No? We do.

Admiring Words. Now the form of delivery is giving us the type of things, which make us really tick. Admiring words. Yum yum indeed. Lay them on us and lay them on thick and often, as we need them.

"Your report is brilliant; you have done a really good job there."
"I love your new hairstyle; it really suits you."
"That new car of yours is superb."
"I find what you say about race relations in this country fascinating."
"Your quarterly results are sensational."

We relish hearing admiring words because others also pick them up (people do this much more than compared to a gesture which is subtler) and as a consequence there is the potential for magnification as others hear what is being said and because of a herd mentality they will join in with the praise and admiration.

With the category of Angry Gesture, we reach the top four and you will immediately notice that the top four consists of negative responses. Anger and tears. These are the reactions that we prize the most because they underline just how powerful we are. It is comparatively easy to get someone to be pleasant, especially an empathic individual because that is the way that they are programmed. They want to be pleasant and kind and nice. On the other hand, causing an empathic person to engage in negative emotions, which manifest through gestures and words, is contrary to their creed. By causing them to react in such a way we are unleashing and demonstrating raw, unadulterated power over these people. That increases our sense of importance, might, omnipotence and superiority. Angry gestures will include frowning, stamping of feet, sticking two fingers up at us, shaking a fist and slamming a door. It includes frustration and annoyance; it includes a person fuming or sending baleful glares. It need not be about shouting with anger. Any form of negativity that is on the spectrum of anger is found in this category. It is all a good form of delivery to us.

Angry Words speak for themselves. We are delighted when the foul language pours from your mouth as you lose your temper with us. We are important because you are focussing this on us and we have really got under your skin by causing you to do this. You may look calm but your words are savage and scathing. This works for us as well.

Tearful Gestures. When we see you sad and miserable we are at the top of our game. You prefer to be happy and cheerful and you will try and maintain this by putting on a brave face. If we can crack through this, then our power is something to behold indeed. Once those tears start to flow then so does the wonderful fuel.

Tearful Words. If you are moved to tell us how miserable and distraught you feel, then we have hit the jackpot. This negative reaction is the top of the tree and we know we have got into the depths of your soul and hurt you.

So, you have the rankings of the proximity of the source and the form of delivery. Two key ingredients in creating fuel for us. It is when these two ingredients are combined that something magical happens and the fuel is created. Thus, if we are in an Internet chat room and someone sends us a message asking us what our age sex and location is, we have a Remote Stranger providing a Neutral Response. It is only a small amount of fuel but it is fuel nevertheless. If this happens several times in an hour, then the effect is multiplied. Now consider this scenario.

1. We are in the study chatting to strangers on the Internet.
(Remote Stranger x Neutral Response moving through to Acknowledgement)

2. A text message arrives from a friend asking how we are.
(Outer Circle Friend x Attentive Words)

3. The landline rings and it is a friend calling to chat who compliments us on a recent deal we tell him or her about.
(Outer Circle Friend x Admiring Words)

4. You come upstairs and tell us that dinner is ready.
(Intimate Partner x Attentive Gesture)

5. We stay in the study so you keep shouting for us to come down for dinner until you come upstairs and confront us about our failure and expressing your displeasure.
(Intimate Partner x (Angry Words and Angry Gestures)

Now, that is only perhaps over the course of an hour. See how much fuel has been created during this time period? You might regard it as plenty but it is only a little to us in the scheme of things because we always need more.

Pause for a moment and consider a typical day for your narcissist. Make a list of those he or she interacts with and the method of interaction and then work out all the various multiples of the generated fuel that occur and understand this. This is just over one day and is substantial in your eyes, yet to us, it is not enough.

You will see from the lists that the most potent form of fuel that arises is from a Former Intimate Partner (Hoover) who engages in Tearful Words. This is the ex-girlfriend who admits in floods of tears down the phone that she misses me. What a jolt of fuel that gives me. Unfortunately, I cannot engineer that to happen all the time. That is why I have to have regard to other sources of fuel. Naturally, I want a combination of the best types of fuel, the highest rankings in the proximity of source and the form of delivery and so much the better if these two ingredients can come from the one individual rather than scattered across different individuals.

Who is going to be always around, who ranks high as proximity of source and is essentially going to be engaged in the provision of tearful gestures and words? Yes, you have guessed, it is the co-dependent. That is why we treasure the co-dependent above all the other providers of fuel and if we can find one and trap one when we are guaranteed a supply of top quality fuel, on a regular basis from someone is unlikely to leave unless we cast them to one side.

Accordingly, you can see that we apply quite a degree of thought into the way we grade the fuel that we seek. We need to ensure that we have one main provider who will be on hand to supply this fuel regularly. An intimate partner is selected owing to their greater emotive state. This individual, if seduced by us, will be an empathic individual and therefore guaranteed to provide us with excellent quality fuel. Ideally, we will then triangulate that person with another prospect who is also an empathic person. It does not always have to be that way, but it is the preferred outcome. With this main source of supply in place, amplified and supported by a triangulating individual we will then put in place lesser sources of fuel that we can keep turning to. These are the family members and colleagues and inner circle friends. Again, these are purposefully arranged so that we have the certainty (or as near as we can muster) that they will be on hand when we want to turn to them to obtain fuel.

After that we will sweep up the fuel wherever we can get it from the lesser sources, such as acquaintances, minions and strangers. They are all helpful and provide additional fuel throughout the course of our day. To give you an idea of how much fuel we gather I am going to ascribe a point value to each element of proximity of the supply and method of delivery.

Proximity of the Source	Points Value
Remote strangers	One
Strangers	Two
Minions	Three
Acquaintances	Four
Colleagues	Five
Outer Circle Friends	Six
Inner Circle Friends	Seven
Family	Eight
Intimate Partners	Nine
Former Intimate Partners (devalue)	Ten
Former Intimate Partners (Hoover)	Fifteen

The F.I.P. (Hoover) is ascribed fifteen points by virtue of the massive potency these people supply. No doubt you are beginning to understand now why it is we try so hard to Hoover you back in. The edifying and invigorating sensation we get even from an awareness response from the F.I.P. (Hoover) is incredible. Next we allocate points to the appropriate types of method of delivery.

Form of Delivery	Points Value
Awareness	One
Neutral Response	Two
Acknowledgement	Three
Loving Gesture	Four
Loving Words	Five
Attentive Gesture	Six
Attentive Words	Seven
Admiring Gesture	Eight
Admiring Words	Nine
Angry Gesture	Ten
Angry Words	Eleven
Tearful Gesture	Twelve
Tearful Words	Thirteen

Thus, when we Hoover you back in when you are our intimate partner and you tearfully express your relief that we have allowed you back in to our life that is **195 fuel points** delivered right there. The equivalent of nearly 49 strangers providing us with a neutral response online. Powerful stuff. I am ascribing a point value to enable you to work out the various permutations so you can gauge what your narcissist is gaining from the activity that he or she is engaging in. It will also help you understand where the best gains are to be obtained by us and you can then make your own appropriate plans. Armed with this information it will help you gain an understanding as to how the narcissist in your life acts and why.

To demonstrate to you just how much fuel can be gathered in a generally ordinary day (and also show you just how much fuel we must gather), let us take the earlier example of a typical day. This time, instead of inserting whether it is positive or negative fuel, I am going to detail the relevant multipliers and point score from each dose of fuel. The proximity of source score comes first and then the form of delivery

You cuddle me **(IP 9 x LG 4 =36)** as I pretend to sleep **(9x2=18)**. I wait until you have gone downstairs and check my mobile 'phone. There are several messages from a potential target, which I am engaged in a text message flirtation with **(4x9=36)**. I send her a reply and there is an instant response **(4x9=36)**. I go downstairs and you greet me asking if I slept well **(9x7=56)**. I complain that the pillows you have bought are too soft and you agree to get me some harder ones **(9x7=56)**. You ask me what I have planned at work **(9x7=56)**. You ask me to get some dry cleaning after work but I refuse and explain I have an existing engagement **(9x7=56)**. I can see my refusal has irked you along with my refusal to explain what my engagement is **(9x10=90)**. You agree to collect the dry cleaning and attend to clearing away the dishes **(9x7=56)**.

I return upstairs and check my phone to find another message from the prospect **(4x9=36)**. I check my e-mails and find there is one thanking me for a deal I have closed **(5x9=45)** a further one which shows my billing to be the highest for the year to date **(5x9=45)** and I append this chart to an e-mail to a competitor with a suitable bragging post **(5x1=5)**. I get dressed and admire my appearance in the mirror. I take a picture and sent it to the prospect, which immediately responds with a complimentary comment **(4x9=36)**.

(I am not even out of the house yet and have already harvested 663 fuel points.)

I have left the bathroom a mess and I have deliberately placed a damp towel on the bed, as I know doing this irritates you **(9x1=9)**. I head downstairs and kiss you good-bye, although I opt to kiss you on the cheek rather than the mouth because I can choose to do this **(9x4=36)**. I get in my car and call a friend to organise a drink later in the week. I spend the first ten minutes of the conversation declaring how well I am doing at work **(6x9=54)** and repeatedly blocking his attempts to tell me his news. His frustration shows in his response. **(6x10=60)**. As I pull up at some traffic lights I notice the young driver next to me admiring my car and he gives me a thumbs up **(2x8=16)**. I overtake several cars on my way to the office **(2x1=2)** and cut one driver up. I see him gesticulate at me from his less expensive car and I laugh in response **(2x10=20)**

On arrival at the office my secretary has a cup of tea waiting for me **(5x6=30)**. During the day I secure a new deal **(4x8=32)**, spread a few lies about a competitor and later overhear him complaining about them although he has no idea where they have come from **(5x11=55)**. A secretary I have not seen before smiles at me **(2x6=12)**. I stop by and chat to her for a while and she is clearly flirting with me **(2x8=16)**. I dress down a junior employee on a flimsy basis and he looks crestfallen **(5x10=50)**. I receive two text messages from you about dinner but I ignore them which I know will make you feel dejected **(9x1=9)** and I continue with a few flirtatious texts with the new prospect **(4x9=36)**. I land a load of work on a junior employee's desk. She starts to complain but I put her in her place **(5x10=50)**. I attend the gym at lunchtime and am met with several admiring glances from male and female attendees as I work our **(2x8=16)**. I return to the office and remark how out of shape a colleague is looking which leaves him fuming since I walk away before he is able to respond. **(5x10=50)**. I telephone you three times and you do not answer so I leave you a nasty voicemail **(9x1=9)**. You ring me back and I have a go at you as you try to apologise **(9x13=117)** and then I hang up on you **(9x1=9)**. You call me twice but I ignore the calls **(9x1=9)** and I also ignore your text messages **(9x1=9)**.

I circulate a congratulatory e-mail I have received from a client and receive several responses acknowledging my achievement **(5x9=45)**. I secure petty cash to pay for my drinks this evening even though it has nothing to do with work **(5x1=5)**. You telephone me and I cut your call off straight away **(9x1=9)**.

I go to a bar straight from work and whilst I am waiting for a female friend I chat-up the bargirl. She is responsive to my overtures and gives me her number **(3x8=24)**. I sit and flirt with my female friend **(7x9=63)** and spend my time explaining how hard my home life is despite all the things that I do because of the way you treat me. She laps it up and is most sympathetic **(7x9=63)**. She asks to meet me next week and I agree. **(7x7=49)**. You call me twice but I deliberately do not answer. **(9x1=9)**. I catch a taxi home and on the way tell a junior employee to head back to work to deliver my car to my house even though he is busy with his family **(5x7=35)**. I accuse the taxi driver of taking the wrong route. He argues back so I don't give him the full fare and take his licence details. **(3x10=30)**. I enter the house and you politely ask where I have been. I regard this as an unnecessary attack so I provoke an argument **(9x10=90)**. I ensconce myself in the study where I engage in some online flirtation **(1x9=9)**. You come to see me to smooth matters over but I provoke another argument, which makes you cry **(9x12=108)**. I continue with my online antics and sign up to a dating sight to punish you for arguing with me **(1x1=1)**.

I heart you head for bed and I decide to watch some porn turning the volume up in the hope you will hear **(9x1=9)** before I noisily head to the spare room so you know that I have decided to sleep in there rather than with you. **(9x1=9)**

That makes a grand total of **1927** fuel points. Substantial isn't it?

A few points are worth noting from this exercise.

1. Notice how insidious our gathering of fuel is. We still harvest fuel when we know that something we do will cause a person to be angry, upset or admiring even though we do not see their reaction. Just the knowledge alone is sufficient to provide us with a boost of fuel.

2. Observe how the fuel points soar when we witness a reaction and how the negative reactions outweigh the positive ones.

3. You are an empathic individual and therefore very good at seeing someone else's point of view and placing yourself in their shoes. Imagine if this was your day. How would you feel after engaging in all this conduct in order to obtain fuel? Exhilarated and powerful? I suspect not. People like you would find the near constant hunt tiring, the frequent abrasiveness wearing and no doubt find much of it shallow and self-serving. We do not. Each instance of fuel makes the flames inside us burn brighter and causes us to feel powerful and omnipotent. Notice how many different instances if fuel gathering take place, of varying types and with different people and you are gaining an insight into how dedicated we must be to the accumulation of fuel. That was just one day. When we awake the following morning, the tank is empty and so it begins all over again. That is how we exist. A day-to-day hunt for fuel. I should imagine that you have often looked at the narcissist you now know that you are engaged with and wondered why they are at war with the world? Why is it that they have to provoke a fight and an argument

over the smallest infraction or indeed over nothing? Now you have your answer. It is all about harvesting the fuel.

4. You will see how the intimate partner provides the most fuel to us. Not only do we obtain this in vast quantities when we are with you, especially when we cause you to speak in a negative fashion, for example calling us names or telling us how upset you are, we gather residual amounts through the day because based on our relationship we know that you will get in touch with us on several occasions (or at least try to) by telephoning, text messaging and/or e-mailing. This is why our kind and me are rarely single. We need that intimate partner to be the mainstay of our fuel supply. Yes, we change them and do so frequently, but we always need that certain somebody in the role of intimate partner.

Now that you see the differing degrees of the type of fuel that we can obtain, this should enable you to understand how the narcissist in your life behaves. If, for example, your narcissist is a social butterfly then they will be gathering a lot of fuel this way from their engagements with people through admiration and flirtation. This may result in them not needing to obtain as much (they will always need to obtain some fuel from you, otherwise why have you around?) fuel from you. Accordingly, if your narcissist is not interacting with you as much as they might ordinarily do so it is because they are securing fuel from alternative sources.

The more outgoing of us will flit from one social organisation to another in order to harvest fuel from a new virgin source. The quality of that fuel will advance over time, as strangers become acquaintances who then become outer circle friends. These people will at first be dazzled by our charm and brilliance and thus their admiring words and gestures will provide us with a lot of fuel. Over time, as normal people do, they become used to us and therefore the admiration will reduce and become less frequent. This is partially offset by the rise in the points of index of the proximity of supplier, moving from 2 points to 4 and then 6. Ultimately however when those people become outer circle friends (any possibly inner circle in a few instances) their admiration will only be so often. We are then faced with a choice. Do we remain and look to increase the form of delivery by causing arguments and upset? If we do, we will only be able to do so for so long before we are eventually turfed out of the organisation. Alternatively, we will choose to go and find a new set of admirers by leaving one organisation and joining another.

This need to acquire fuel and also the higher graded fuel can result in areas of our lives being chaotic. We make and break friends readily because of our need to derive the higher type of fuel that comes with negative words and gestures, but this will come at a cost of the friendship. We do not care about that. We are not programmed to be concerned about how others might feel about the way we treat them. We are entitled to do as we please and this is all because we must obtain fuel.

The narcissist in your life may shift jobs frequently and appear to have a chaotic approach to employment. Part of this arises from our sense of entitlement and high-handed treatment of others, but essentially it boils down to the need to obtain fuel. The repeated need to obtain fuel and of a negative variety means that my kind engage in conduct which falls outside normative behaviour and the consequence of this is that we have to move jobs. In addition, or alternatively, the once admiring audience has become used to us and therefore does not provide us with the admiration that we crave and so we must depart and seek out fresh admirers.

This is why we operate through a pattern of seduction and devaluation. When we seduce a person, be it into our friendship, our confidence at work or intimately, we at first draw deep on the loving, attentive and admiring words and gestures that flow from the new recruit. These are freely given. As with any normal relationship, the novelty factor diminishes. In a normal relationship the dynamic would settle down into a long-standing and settled one, based on understanding and respect (I hear this said many times by others). In our relationships, the diminution of the novelty factor means less fuel. We either seek out new ones (which takes additional energy to do) or more likely we shift tack and decide that since we must extort a reaction from you, we may as well go for the negative ones. This means greater fuel from us, it allows us to punish you for failing to keep up the supply of positive reactions and thus the devaluation begins. This also serves to confuse you so that you remain with us trying to fix matters. This will cause the resumption of positive reactions from you. This is welcomed but we have enjoyed tasting the fuel from provoking a negative reaction from you and therefore we want more. We become greedy. We want you admiring, attentive and loving but we also want to provoke anger and upset too. This is why you are then thrown into a spin cycle of push and pull, up and down, pleasantness and nastiness. It is all a product of our need to acquire fuel.

You may be involved with a narcissist who stays at home all day, not wishing to expend energy in hunting out fuel from other sources, or it may be, by reason of illness, that he or she cannot go elsewhere. The advent of extensive technological communication will allow the provision of some fuel throughout the day but it will be on the lower end of the spectrum. In such an instance, expect when you walk in through the door after a hard day at work, to be subjected to provocation, which seeks to elicit angry and/or tearful responses from you. Your narcissist is very hungry for fuel, having just about been sustained on titbits through the day. Now he or she wants a prime and succulent steak and you are that steak. They cannot accept admiration, attentiveness and love since those reactions alone, even from an intimate partner, are now not enough for him or her. They need to drill into the seam from which the top-grade fuel will spill by arguing with you, frustrating you and upsetting you.

Accordingly, utilising the exercise in understanding where we get our fuel from and how we subsequently grade it is a powerful tool for you to learn about. You should spend some time making a note of how your narcissist gathers fuel and then score it. You should then start to see certain patterns emerging. If you are largely left alone, then the fuel will be coming from elsewhere. Does your narcissist suddenly decide he or she wants to attend a family event? Put your hard hat on. They are looking to cause an explosion and gather a lot of fuel. Stay-at-home narc? Early evening rows and arguments are ahead. By mapping the nature of the supply your narcissist obtains and scoring it accordingly, you will be able to have an idea of what he or she is up to and what might be coming. It may not be pleasant but if you know it is on the horizon you can take steps to deal with it. You may decide to absent yourself forcing the narcissist to obtain fuel a different way but at least it is not at your expense. You may realise you need to keep the admiration flowing (even when it feels a strange thing to do when you have been together a long time) but this may just prevent the narcissist seeking out the negative fuel or at least less often.

By understanding and observing what our sources of fuel actually are, you will go a long way to gaining insight into why we behave the way that we do, what it is that drives us, why we act as we do at certain times when it appears to lack logic and it will provide you with a method of deciding what you might be able to do to ameliorate the effects of our behaviour for your own sake and those around you.

What Does Fuel Do For Us?

You understand what fuel is, where we obtain it from and the methods by which we do so. You understand that it is central to our existence and that our need for it is vast and daily. We must next consider what is it that the fuel does for a narcissist.

You may think, by referring to the method of delivery described above that the provision of fuel must make us feel loved, attended to or admired. You would be wrong. You give out those feelings. By slipping your arms around us and telling us that you love us, you are showing you feel love. We do not feel it. By doing our laundry, making our meals and keeping the house tidy, you do not make us feel attended on, but rather that is what you are doing. When you say how brilliant we are at our job or send us an appreciative look when we show you the new watch that we have bought, we do not feel admiration. That is what you are giving out.

On the occasions that you become frustrated or you shout, we do not feel bad for having made you feel this way. We do not feel a need to understand how you are feeling and to try and make you feel better by removing the anger. Your tears show us that you are upset but we are not going to make them go away by comforting you.

All of your reactions, be they as a consequence of gestures or words make us feel one thing; powerful. Inside us there is a single flame that is always burning. It is not very bright and gives off little heat but it is there. It is like a pilot light that is ever present, ready to be amplified and increased and this happens through the provision of fuel. When you provide us with fuel, this flame grows. It burns brighter and the heat it gives off becomes greater. The flame becomes a fire, which becomes a furnace. With the addition of more fuel, the furnace becomes a conflagration and then an inferno. Searing flames dance and twirl as the jets of flame play onto it, the orange flames reaching higher and higher, burning with a greater intensity as the air shimmers from the heat haze. The bigger the fire the more powerful we feel. It surges through us, it edifies and invigorates us. This fire gives us power.

Why is this power so important to us? By feeling powerful we are able to do as we please, when we please and how we please. This fulfils our sense of entitlement. By creating this power, it furnishes us with the tools to extend our charm and draw in fresh victims. The extension of this power provides us with the means to assert our superiority and ensure that we have control over you. The power enables us to domineer, subjugate and continue with all our machinations that keep people in their places as appliances for us. It is a remorseless cycle. We need our fuel to feel powerful. By being made powerful we then have the means to keep you and others within our control and thus keep providing us with fuel.

This is how we differ from you. From what I have read and experienced about your kind, you gain a sense of purpose and well being from conducting yourself in a manner that is caring and giving. You believe in your essential goodness and that of other people. Yes, you grow tired, upset and angry but all your responses are normal ones, which are entirely expected when people are subjected to a lack of sleep, stress or hurtful comments. Our reactions do not equate with yours. All of our responses are designed in order to bring about the provision of fuel. You do something for somebody because it makes you feel good inside to care for another person. You gain something, be it self-esteem, self-worth or "that warm feeling inside" by having a care for another person, helping someone who is in need or giving something of you to another person. This might be dedicating yourself to bringing up a child, caring for a sick relative, volunteering for a charity, teaching at a special school and such like. All of these giving acts generate a reward for you in terms of self-esteem and feeling worthwhile.

We cannot do that. It is not the way that we are programmed. As above, I provided an example of a typical day for both you and I. In the first instance I determined the fuel that you gathered from your interaction with people and the number of instances was far lower than compared to the situation for me. With the addition of the matrix of fuel points, the gulf was huge. In the interests of balance, but also to enable you to understand what fuel does for us and why we need it, let us revisit that typical day. On this occasion, I will strip out all the instances of the ways in which I garnered negative fuel. Let us assume that on this particular day, I do not engage in any behaviour, which would gather negative fuel, and I do nothing instead. I only keep in those instances where I gather positive fuel. Here is what it would look like.

You cuddle me **(IP 9 x LG 4 =36)** ~~as I pretend to sleep **(9x2=18)**.~~ I wait until you have gone downstairs and check my mobile 'phone. There are several messages from a potential target, which I am engaged in a text message flirtation with **(4x9=36)**. I send her a reply and there is an instant response **(4x9=36)**. I go downstairs and you greet me asking if I slept well **(9x7=56)**. ~~I complain that the pillows you have bought are too soft and you agree to get me some harder ones **(9x7=56)**.~~ You ask me what I have planned at work **(9x7=56)**. ~~You ask me to get some dry cleaning after work but I refuse and explain I have an existing engagement **(9x7=56)**. I can see my refusal has irked you along with my refusal to explain what my engagement is **(9x10=90)**.~~ You agree to collect the dry cleaning and attend to clearing away the dishes **(9x7=56)**.

I return upstairs and check my phone to find another message from the prospect **(4x9=36)**. I check my e-mails and find there is one thanking me for a deal I have closed **(5x9=45)** a further one which shows my billing to be the highest for the year to date **(5x9=45)** ~~and I append this chart to an e-mail to a competitor with a suitable bragging post **(5x1=5)**~~. I get dressed and admire my appearance in the mirror. I take a picture and sent it to the prospect, which immediately responds with a complimentary comment **(4x9=36)**.

~~I have left the bathroom a mess and I have deliberately placed a damp towel on the bed, as I know doing this irritates you **(9x1=9)**.~~ I head downstairs and kiss you good-bye, although I opt to kiss you on the cheek rather than the mouth because I can choose to do this **(9x4=36)**. I get in my car and call a friend to organise a drink later in the week. I spend the first ten minutes of the conversation declaring how well I am doing at work **(6x9=54)** ~~and repeatedly blocking his attempts to tell me his news. His frustration shows in his response. **(6x10=60)**.~~ As I pull up at some traffic lights I notice the young driver next to me admiring my car and he gives me a thumbs up **(2x8=16)**. ~~I overtake several cars on my way to the office **(2x1=2)** and cut one driver up. I see him gesticulate at me from his less expensive car and I laugh in response **(2x10=20)**~~

On arrival at the office my secretary has a cup of tea waiting for me **(5x6=30)**. During the day I secure a new deal **(4x8=32)**, ~~spread a few lies about a competitor and later overhear him complaining about them although he has no idea where they have come from **(5x11=55)**.~~ A secretary I have not seen before smiles at me **(2x6=12)**. I stop by and chat to her for a while and she is clearly flirting with me **(2x8=16)**. ~~I dress down a junior employee on a flimsy basis and he looks crestfallen **(5x10=50)**. I receive two text messages from you about dinner but I ignore them which I know will make you feel dejected **(9x1=9)**~~ and I continue with a few flirtatious texts with the new prospect **(4x9=36)**. ~~I land a load of work on a junior employee's desk. She starts to complain but I put her in her place **(5x10=50)**.~~ I attend the gym at lunchtime and am met with several admiring glances from male and female attendees as I work our **(2x8=16)**. ~~I return to the office and remark how out of shape a colleague is looking which leaves him fuming since I walk away before he is able to respond. **(5x10=50)**. I telephone you three times and you do not answer so I leave you a nasty voicemail **(9x1=9)**. You ring me back and I have a go at you as you try to apologise **(9x13=117)** and then I hang up on you **(9x1=9)**. You call me twice but I ignore the calls **(9x1=9)** and I also ignore your text messages **(9x1=9)**.~~

I circulate a congratulatory e-mail I have received from a client and receive several responses acknowledging my achievement **(5x9=45)**. ~~I secure petty cash to pay for my drinks this evening even though it has nothing to do with work **(5x1=5)**. You telephone me and I cut your call off straight away **(9x1=9)**.~~

I go to a bar straight from work and whilst I am waiting for a female friend I chat-up the bargirl. She is responsive to my overtures and gives me her number **(3x8=24)**. I sit and flirt with my female friend **(7x9=63)** and spend my time explaining how hard my home life is despite all the things that I do because of the way you treat me. She laps it up and is most sympathetic **(7x9=63)**. She asks to meet me next week and I agree. **(7x7=49)**. ~~You call me twice but I deliberately do not answer. **(9x1=9)**. I catch a taxi home and on the way tell a junior employee to head back to work to deliver my car to my house even though he is busy with his family **(5x7=35)**. I accuse the taxi driver of taking the wrong route. He argues back so I don't give him the full fare and take his licence details. **(3x10=30)**. I enter the house and you politely ask where I have been. I regard this as an unnecessary attack so I provoke an argument **(9x10=90)**.~~ I ensconce myself in the study where I engage in some online flirtation **(1x9=9)**. ~~You come to see me to smooth matters over but I provoke another argument, which makes you cry~~ **(9x12=108)**. ~~I continue with my online antics and sign up to a dating sight to punish you for arguing with me~~ **(1x1=1)**.

~~I heart you head for bed and I decide to watch some porn turning the volume up in the hope you will hear~~ **(9x1=9)** ~~before I noisily head to the spare room so you know that I have decided to sleep in there rather than with you.~~ **(9x1=9)**

In the previous example, I racked up a total of **1927** fuel points. This time it is reduced to **1030** fuel points, nearly cut in half. You may consider that this is a better state of affairs, since I have removed negative responses and still I have been able to harvest fuel. The level of fuel that has been collected is not nearly enough to provide me with the power that I require and desire. You may then suggest instead that if that is the case that I reduce the deficit by continuing to garner positive fuel. I need to obtain more attention, more loving behaviour and more admiration. I suspect you will reason that by at least obtaining positive fuel to address the deficit we are less likely to hurt people by taking this route. In making that suggestion, I want you to go back over the example given above and identify the instances where I did something positive which would be regarded as benefiting the other person or other people. What did you conclude?

1. The text message exchange with the potential prospect. No doubt my sugarcoated texts will have pleased her, but it was only done to ensure I received similar messages in return. As an empathic individual, I do not think that you would regard them as particularly giving in nature.

2. Declaring how well I am doing at work. It might not be regarded as negative as such but it certainly was not done to make anyone else feel better about themselves. It was boastful behaviour.

3.   I secure a new deal. That might generate additional income for the company but that is not what concerns me. I am far more interested in how good it makes me look.

4.   The flirtation with the new secretary, doing similar online and also in person with the female friend. Again, they doubtless felt good at this behaviour but once again that was not the aim. The aim was to get them to pay me compliments and cause them to admire me and give me attention.

5.   The congratulatory e-mail from a client. Again, it may not be negative but it is purely showing-off and designed to cause people to comment on my achievement.

The only instance in an entire day where I do something for someone else is where I kiss you and even then it is on the cheek and not on the mouth in an attempt to wound you. On this occasion you did not react and you were content with the show of affection from me.

In the entirety of the day, I only do one thing for someone else. Everything else is either of a negative nature or where it is positive, it is about showing-off or is designed to gather a positive reaction for me. I have no interest in whether the other person feels better about himself or herself because I have flirted with them. You might also question the fact that I am engaging in flirtation with others when I am in a relationship already.

Accordingly, if you instructed me to strip out the negative fuel I would protest at the deficiency that arises. If you suggest to me that I gather additional fuel through positive actions, two problems present themselves.

1.   Would you want me gathering these positive reactions by showing off, boasting, flirting and only doing something when I know it will give me a positive reaction?

2.   Realistically that day appeared pretty full. Where else might I have gathered positive fuel? Possibly you suggest that I spend the evening with you and gather various loving, attentive and admiring gestures and words from a multiplier of nine rather than a seven or a two or a one. That of course presupposes that you would provide this on a similar scale bearing in mind that we have been together a while and your effectiveness at doling out positive fuel has been reduced. It also means that I would have to expend additional energy to try and cause you to provide this positive fuel.

Your suggested alternative will not result in me being able to gather sufficient fuel and this will reduce my power. This leaves me with less methods and capabilities for manipulation of those around me, resulting in a potential loss of control and a subsequent further reduction of fuel. This is not something I can countenance. It is far, far easier for me to provoke an argument with you and send the fuel level racing and imbuing me with power. Now do you see why we do it?

This scenario and explanation should also demonstrate to you why it is that we do not go out of our way to behave in a giving and caring manner. It might generate some positive fuel for us, for example, if we look after you when you are ill and you express your gratitude by telling us how much that you love us, then positive fuel of **9x5** arises equalling **45** points. That is not powerful but nor is it weak. The problem with this is that we have to expend energy in looking after you and this means that the 45 points that might be gathered are really halved or even quartered. Why would we do this with such a measly points haul when we could be out with our mistress who is telling us how brilliant we are in devising a new scheme at work (**9x9** with no reduction for energy expenditure). Alternatively, we might stay with you and berate you for being ill so you become upset with us and tell us how uncaring we are (**9x13** and we haven't even had to step outside of the house).

You look after somebody who is ill and you are pleased to see his or her gratitude at being cared for. There is no such thing as an empathy point. You do not do the things that you do for the sake of gathering your fuel and in doing so seeking the best type of empathy fuel. You do it for the good of the act in itself. Yes, you feel pleased with yourself and it gives you a sense of purpose, but they are by products of what you do. You do not need to do it to define yourself or to gain power. You do it because you want to and you believe in doing such acts.

We do not have this luxury. If we spent our time carrying out empathic acts (we may not feel it but we have seen you do them so we know how to mimic showing empathy) then the fuel, we would draw from such acts would be at the lower end of the scale and this would be diluted by the energy we expend in doing it. Not only do we not carry out empathic behaviours because we are not naturally empathic (or empathic at all) it is also because it serves no purpose to us. It is a wasted act. It does not gather any or enough fuel for us and therefore it denies us power. If we have our power reduced, we cannot maintain our superiority. We are unable to control others and we are denied the opportunity to carry out our manipulative behaviours. Our very existence begins to crumble.

Fuel equals power equals control equals fuel. Round and round it goes. We need the fuel to create power, which in turn provides us with the devices by which we can remain in control and subsequently obtain more fuel. It is a perfect cycle and one, which we are dedicated to.

There is another answer to the question of what does obtaining fuel do for us? It is linked to the provision of power. Fuel enables us, through the gaining of power, to maintain our construct.

The construct is what we create in order to demonstrate to the world how brilliant and magnificent we are. In order to achieve this, we must select various character traits and attributes of those around us in order to commandeer those traits for ourselves and in turn enable us to fashion the construct. We need to take the fragments, pieces and shards from many other people. A sliver of intellect from the academic we have met, the shard of sporting achievement from our school friend who is now a professional sportsman. We take a chunk of beauty from the lady who lives across the road who is always so magnificently turned out and attired. We purloin that fragment of comedic ability from a colleague at work who regularly has people in stitches of laughter. A dash of success from him, a piece of knowledge from her, several sections of bravery from that fire-fighter, a segment of artistic excellence from our cousin, an element of style from someone else. We gather all of these constituent pieces and from them we build the construct. It imprisons the creature inside (more about that beast later) and also shows to the world how talented and marvellous that we are. We must fashion this construct for otherwise we cannot survive in this cruel and harsh world. You might regard it as a mask, or a cloak or a tower. Whichever object suits your purposes feel free to select it. Whichever one you choose it is a construct that has a dual purpose. It imprisons the creature and shows the world what we really consider ourselves to be.

The maintenance of the construct enables us to charm and seduce. This means that we can gather fresh and new victims from whom we can extract further fuel. We can show off our brilliance in order to force and extort others to give us fuel. I am aware of why I do this through the force of my own intellect and the guiding observations from those treating me, Dr E and Dr O. Regular readers will be well acquainted with the good doctors. We all know that the construct must be built.

Not only must it be built but also it must be maintained. The only thing that can keep its thousands of constituent parts together is having the power to keep it all in place and intact. The only way for us to have enough power to do this is to be provided with sufficient fuel. If we do not have the fuel, we lose power and risk the edifice tumbling to the ground. We cannot countenance that happening as that will result in our destruction.

Consider for a moment a skyscraper. The materials used in its construction are substantial. Putting those materials in place takes vast amounts of time, money and energy. Just in the same way as it is takes vast amounts of fuel to create the power to build our construct. Even when the skyscraper has been completed, it takes a lot of maintenance. Checks must be taken on its structural integrity. Running repairs must be effected where damage has been found. The walls and roof must remain impervious to the elements, to the wind and the rain that howl around it, seeking to find a way in. The windows need to be cleaned, the interior swept and vacuumed, polished and maintained. Marble must shine, the electrics must be overhauled, and the pipes and conduits that provide the various utilities need to be maintained. For that skyscraper to remain intact again takes considerable amounts of time, money and energy. Similarly, for our construct to remain in place and not fall part, it takes considerable amounts of power, which has been generated by this fuel.

We need power to build the construct.

We need power to maintain the construct.

We need power so the construct can maintain our brilliance.

We need power so the construct can imprison the creature.

All of this power needs fuel, fuel and more fuel.

This is what fuel does for us. It provides us with power, which in turn enables us to build and maintain the construct. The construct keeps the beast at bay and enables us to portray the image we want to the world so we can seduce more people and extract more fuel from them. Round and round it goes. Never ending.

This is what fuel does for us. This is why we need so much of it. This is why we cannot spend our time committing acts that care for others and are acts of giving. To do so will not generate the fuel we need. This is why we are beholden to seducing you and others to provide us with both positive and negative fuel. This is what we must do each and every day, without interruption and respite. There is no end to it, no ultimate outcome. The gathering of fuel is what we need for the power to maintain the construct and in doing so preserve our existence.

Why Not Stop?

This may be the question, which has now formed in your minds. You understand what our fuel is, how much we need it and why we have to behave in the way that we do to harvest as much fuel as we possibly can to maintain our power. However, you consider that this is perhaps only serving to perpetuate something, which is not actually any good for us. I have heard such an accusation on several occasions. Why keep adhering to a way of life which has you trapped in this endless cycle? Why submit to it? Why keep doing it? Why don't you just stop and seek a different way of existing? Yes, these questions have been asked of me many times from puzzled therapists through to frustrated family members and perplexed lovers. What is stopping us from putting an end to this arrangement? I shall explain.

The first point to consider is that we are addicted to this state of affairs. In the same way that an alcoholic wants and needs an alcoholic drink and the drug addict requires his or fix. It is similar to the gym bunny that spends every night on the treadmill because he or she is addicted to the way exercise makes them feel or the obese person who guzzles litres of fizzy pop every day. It is a question of addiction.

I love feeling powerful. I love being superior. I love people admiring me. I love exerting control over people so they behave, as I want. I love being able to manipulate them to do my bidding. I love the way I can make a person feel ecstatic, miserable, terrified and upset. I love being a god. Many normal people would relish the opportunity to feel this powerful. I know you will not since you are most likely an empathic person and an obsession with power and its effects is not something that will appeal to you. You tend to be the antidote to the power from what I have observed. Leaving you aside for the moment however, many normal people would enjoy wielding power in the way that I do. I am sure you can think of examples or you can consider people that you have actually known who, once they have been provided with a little power, they crave more. Once they have had that taste of being in a position of power and they see what can be achieved by wielding it, then he or she will want to be given more power or to exercise it for longer. As Lord Acton sagely put it, "Power corrupts and absolute power corrupts absolutely."

You can conjure up the examples. There is the teacher who is able to keep an entire class behind after school owing to the behaviour of one pupil. The promoted employee who ensures that his former peers now undertake all of the dirty work. The person who is put in charge of the allocation of tickets for a special event who decides to allow his friends to attend at the exclusion of some long standing members of the society for whom the event has been organised. There are many examples of individuals being provided with power, even at a lowly level and they soon relish the fact they have this power in their hands. Knowing this, imagine how it feels when you exude power each and every day?

Contemplate what it must feel like when you can make somebody fall in love with you, lend you money, sing your praises, want to live with you, make your meals and attend to all your domestic chores and dedicate themselves to making you happy? Consider the power that can be wielded to cause someone to forgo all of their friends for you or shun their family in order to please you. How about being able to exercise such power that you can affect somebody's emotions and sanity? You are able to control them and have them at your beck and call. Imagine having the power to do as you please without any concern for repercussion or consequence? Think about what it must be like to know that you are special and elevated and this is why you have been blessed with these abilities? I would defy anybody who deemed themselves normal not to be affected by being able to wield such power. Once they have it they will cling on to it and fight to retain it. Why should my kind and me be any different?

The nature of the power that we have is such that it is utterly addictive. I cannot remember a time when I was not able to manipulate people. Of course it began, like these types of developed abilities do with the smallest of influences. I could make my sister do what I wanted when I was younger. I could not do any wrong in the eyes of some. I had them believe everything that I said. I progressed and found I was able to turn friend against friend. I was able to lie, cheat and steal with impunity, taking anything I wanted and being so adept at blaming others and keeping up a smokescreen of deception that I was never held to account.

I learned from the best and was given this insight into how one can control another person so they give you what you want. Many people are easily led. They lack the fibre to resist the lure of those of us with charisma. These people want to believe the fairy tale. They are convinced that there will be a happy ever after and as a consequence they make themselves vulnerable to the power of suggestion and manipulation. As I grew so did my power and with it came the realisation that so long as I had this power I would be safe. It could not touch me. I was able to keep it at bay.

I have evolved and grown with power in my hands and I can never let that feeling be relinquished. I must have it. I know no other way and why should I contemplate another way when this one always works for me. Yes, it is never ending but it works. I seek fuel, I gain fuel and I wield power. It is a straightforward equation. During the interaction with those treating me, Dr E and Dr O, we have touched on why I do not stop doing what I do. The conversation that we had went something like this. Dr E began the conversation.

"Let's talk some more about what you call fuel."

"By all means," I responded.

"We have talked at length about the manner in which you obtain this fuel and we have spent a couple of sessions establishing why you need this fuel. I should add I do not think that those discussions are complete."

"Well you wouldn't would you when you are getting paid so well by the hour would you doctor?" I answered and smiled. Dr E ignored my comment and carried on.

"We will continue to discuss the question of fuel and the part it plays in your life. I would like you to consider today whether you would ever contemplate stopping your pursuit of fuel?"

"No I would not," I answered straight away.

"What? Not even contemplate it?"

"No. I mean, I will discuss the idea with you if that is what you would like to do," I continued, "but I cannot contemplate seriously stopping my pursuit of fuel."

"Why not?"

"It is all I know."

Dr E nodded and made a note.

"Indulge me for a moment or two. What if I said to you that there was another way you could live, what would you think of that?"

"Another way besides gathering fuel?" I clarified. He nodded. I paused for a moment.

"I would tell you that I am not interested."

"Why?"

"Because this is all I know."

"Indeed, but tell me why you would not be interested in a different method."

"I wouldn't be interested because it would not be as effective as what I do now."

"How would you know if you have not tried an alternative method?" pressed Dr E.

"The method I adopt has to be the most effective. If it were not, I would not be doing it. I always adopt the best way of doing something."

"Is that so?" asked Dr E.

I nodded.

"I understand your viewpoint, but again, indulge me. Let us say, purely for the sake of example, that there is actually a different and better way of conducting your life that does not involve the need to gather fuel. Accept for the moment that there is such a way. Would you be inclined to want to try it, bearing in mind you just admitted that you always adopt the best way of doing something."

I hesitated. I should not have said that I always adopt the best way. That has chained me to always seeking out the best way even if it contradicts my stance.

"I may want to try it, but I could not."

Dr E paused and looked at me.

"Did I just hear you say that there was something you could not do?"

I nodded.

"Why?" he asked.

"I have an existing method. It works. It provides me with fuel and that is how I survive. Even if believed you that there was a better method, and I don't by the way, but I am showing willing by going along with your example, "Dr E nodded in approval at my rare concession, "I could not adopt it because I am too heavily invested in the way that I operate now. Your new method is likely to expend my energy and I do not want that. I know what works and I will stick with it."

Dr E scribbled away in his notebook as I waited for his response.

"What would you say if I suggested that you were addicted to fuel?"

"Addicted?" I repeated.

"Yes, addicted. You see, I suggest to you that you have a compulsive engagement in rewarding stimuli even though it has adverse consequences. I regard your behaviour as exhibiting addiction because the stimuli that is fuel is both reinforcing and rewarding."

"Go on," I said interested in what Dr E had to say.

"you obtain fuel and this behaviour in doing so is reinforcing in that you will seek repeated and frequent exposure to this fuel. It is also rewarding in that you regard fuel as something desirable. Take for example somebody who is addicted to cocaine. This stimulus is regarded as rewarding because the user feels powerful and superior and the user reinforces the stimuli because he seeks repeated use of it. You keep looking for fuel and you perceive a reward that arises from you obtaining it, namely the power you experience which you have described to me on a previous occasion."

"I cannot disagree with that, much as I would like to," I responded.

Dr E made a further note.

"You exhibit the classic hallmarks of addiction. You have impaired control over your behaviour in order to secure your fuel. You will do almost anything to anybody to secure it. You are preoccupied with it. When we discussed a typical day, nearly every sentence you said in describing what went on in your day revolved around you obtaining fuel. Finally, you continue to seek fuel despite the consequences of doing so. Lost relationships, broken friendships, other people being emotionally injured by your pursuit of fuel and so on."

"I see," I replied, "so I am grouped amidst the smackheads, the drunks, the sex addicts, shopaholics and the teens wired to their Xboxes am I?"

"In essence yes. Those who are addicted in those categories activate their reward system through their compulsive behaviour be it drinking or engaging in sexual activity."

"So are you suggesting that being addicted to fuel," I began.

"I would suggest that you are addicted to the power which the fuel provides," interjected Dr E.

"Very well, are you suggesting that being addicted to this power which arises from the fuel is why I will not countenance an alternative way of living?"

Dr E made another note and I swear that a smile began to form on his lips but he chased it away.

"Correct. Your addiction is so intense that it governs all of your thoughts and behaviours. Your addiction to this power is so ingrained you will not do anything else nor will you consider doing anything else."

I was pleased that Dr E had taken such an interest in me and his attentiveness was rewarding. I was itching however to try and provoke him since I was agreeing with what he was suggesting and I did not want him to think that he had gained any advantage over me by so doing.

"I could stop, if I wanted to, but I choose not to," I said.

"So you believe you do have a choice?"

"Of course I do. I always have a choice. As I have told you before doctor, I make the decisions. I am the doer. I am not done to."

"Yes you have. So, you believe you could stop seeking fuel if you wanted to?"

"Absolutely."

"Interesting, I would suggest that you do not have such a choice and that you are unable to choose a different method."

Excellent, he was wanting to debate with me. I was getting under his skin a little. That was what I wanted. It mattered little to me that I was now lying. I had to get him irritated and frustrated so that I could obtain some fuel from him. If you have paid attention and you are now following my recollections by virtue of applying the fuel points system, you no doubt have spotted that I am trying to elicit an angry gesture or angry words from Dr E. Where would a therapist come in the proximity of the supply however? He is something of a minion in that he provides a service, but the intimate nature of the discussion would rank him higher. He is not an intimate partner since we are not bound together in that way, nor are we that involved with one another. He is not a colleague because there is not that work-placed dynamic. I would place the good doctor as an outer circle friend with the potential to become an inner circle friend, so all in all he is a decent ranking within the proximity of the supply.

I need not repeat the rest of that particular session with Dr E as it continued in the vein of me arguing against his hypothesis (even though it made sense to me) purely in order to try and extract some fuel from him. On that occasion he kept his cool in his words and therefore my fuel was a combination of attentive words and angry gestures (he rolled his eyes a few times and sighed in irritation).

However, other than the fuel that I gathered from that particular session, the important item was that I learned that I have an addiction to power. I accept that. I am not willing to treat that addiction as it serves me a considerable purpose. Where I do differ with Dr E is that he made reference to my addiction being about short-term gain with long-term deleterious consequences. I explained that I did not see any downside in the long-term. I would not get liver disease like the alcoholic or an enlarged heart like the cocaine addict. Dr E suggested that the downside was the inability to form deep-seated and long lasting, productive relationships with people at every level of life. He added that a downside was the frequent chaos that was exhibited in my life and the impact that had on those around me, ranging from family to colleagues to partners. He began to reel off other downsides that he saw from my addiction to power and the relentless pursuit of fuel but I tuned him out at this stage as he was beginning to drone on. Each time I just batted his concern away by telling him that there was no long-term downside for me. He had not suggested anything that affected my physical or mental health and as for all the other consequences he referred to, including relationships et al, I just explained that I did not care about those consequences. I do not. Therefore, there is no downside. He tried to make me see an alternative but I was not convinced.

Accordingly, in answer to the question of why do I not just stop this pursuit of fuel and the power it provides, one part of the answer is that I am unable to do so because I am addicted to it. The second part to this answer concerns the fact that I am unwilling to stop precisely because of the consequences that will arise if I do. I am not willing at all to suffer those consequences. There are a number of consequences and one substantial one, which I will be discussing in a degree of detail. The consequences are as follows: -

1. I lose power;

2. I lose prestige and standing;

3. My superiority is challenged;

4. I lose control over other people;

5. The construct would begin to fall apart;

6. The loss of the construct will lead to the loss of the tools and mechanisms by which I am able to gather future fuel; and

7. The imprisonment of the creature will be compromised.

I think you are able to understand how items one through to six affect me. It is the final consequence I wish to write about further.

The Loss of the Prison

This chapter details my absolute fear that f I stopped gathering fuel. I would lose power. The construct would crumble and its encompassing prison would be lost. I have explored this further with Dr O and it is through many sessions with her that I am able to articulate my concern as to what will happen if I lose the imprisoning effect of the construct.

A long time ago I hurled what I refer to as the creature into the prison that is the construct. Like some fevered bricklayer I set about fashioning a prison that would keep the creature out of sight, out of hearing and out of mind. Whilst the brick layer places a brick, adds mortar, then another brick, more mortar and then a brick on top of the two already laid, I built this prison with the shards and fragments from those around me, as I have described above. Everything was held in place by my power.

So long as I had fuel it would generate the power to keep the prison intact. It is akin to having sufficient coal available by which one could generate electricity, which powers an electric fence and keeps the offenders from scaling that fence. If there is no more coal the power is cut and the fence can now be scaled. The offenders escape. I made this prison a long time ago. I will admit that it was rudimentary. There were gaps through which the creature would hiss and shout, its horrible voice drifting outwards to remind me of all the things that I would rather not be. Occasionally, one of its claws would breach the construct. The scrabbling claw would flail around on the end of a scrawny arm as it sought to wrench other pieces of the prison away. It became a running battle. The creature tried to tear down that which I had created as I desperately sought to repair the damage and patch up the holes that it had punched. Some days it pulled down whole sections and reminded me of that which I would rather not contemplate.

The fearful features staring at me as I tried to wrench my gaze away from those hollow eyes. Frantically I sought out fuel to restore the power and cement the shards, fragments and sections back into place. I lashed out at those around me, demanding their reactions so that the fuel would flow once again and I could rest, if only for a moment, chest heaving and heart pounding.

Over time as I watched the way you and your kind behaved and I learned and observed and I mimicked, I began to hone my skills. Through their repeated application, I began to polish my skills at seduction so that more and more people fell under my spell. I became more adept at extracting the positive fuel that flows from love, attention and admiration from these people. Friends, colleagues, acquaintances and lovers all became subjected to my influence. The more I exercised this growing skill, the more powerful it became so that the fuel flowed free and fast. This enabled me to add to the construct so that I acquired more enticing sections and fascinating fragments to cement together.

My reach grew all the more expansive as I sought out fresh victims for my seductions. I plucked them from bars, from work, from childhood and from the social networks I had plugged into. I soon enhanced my skill in the dark art of devaluation and realised just how potent the fuel was that was garnered when I subjected someone to the denigration and distress of my vicious put-downs and mistreatment. The fuel kept flowing and my power rose so that the construct grew mightier, higher and more magnificent. Build it and they will come. And they did. This shining edifice rose like a beacon to which the good and the empathic flocked, eager to be a part of the enticing world the construct promised. With every conquest another layer was added to the creation and its radiance grew.

The greater the opulence of the construct grew, the greater the demands that arose in order to keep it maintained. The marvellous creation began to take on a life of its own, requiring more and more power to keep it intact and thus the hunt for fuel became more urgent and more intense. Deep within the bowels of the construct cowered the creature. I sensed that I had cowed him into some degree of submission. The thickness of the walls of the construct muffled his pain-filled howls until they could no longer be heard. The holes could no longer be smashed into it and the frenetic scratching seemed to diminish. I am no fool though. I know that he lurks still. I do not always hear his protests, catcalls and admonishments but I know he will still utter them, the sardonic words echoing about his chamber of imprisonment. It only takes a lapse of my quest for fuel for the power to ebb and then he will strike, rabidly tearing away the segments of my construct as he tries to surface and wound me with a yellowed nail before bursting out of the construct.

What is the creature? I have come to realise that this is what I would rather not confront nor contemplate. It is the manifestation of all my weaknesses. The weaknesses that I was given by those who ought to have known better and done more to prevent their accumulation. Fear and weakness are the food and drink for the creature. I understand from Dr O that everyone has one of these feckless beasts but it is only those that are like me who are tormented to such a degree that we have chosen to banish the creature into the construct. It is not for us to try and confront it. If I were to do that, it would consume me and I would cease to exist, in the way that I want to exist. In order to prevent this craven creature from governing my life and assimilating me into its awful existence, I chose to create the construct. This was my way of defending myself against the very thing that represents the worst of me and the things that I do not want to be reminded of. Every weakness, failure, disappointment, flaw, frailty, foible, blemish and shortcoming is contained within that creature. It is the master of my imperfection and to allow it blinking into the light of day is to allow the world to see all of those defects. I must not allow that to happen. Ever. By consigning it to the bondage of my construct I am able to be that which I want the world to see. Popular, strong, successful and all conquering. That is what the world wants from me. That is what the world admires and desires.

Accordingly, this is the second reason as to why I cannot stop doing what I do. If I stop harvesting fuel, then I will suffer a power cut. The construct will then surely fall apart and the creature will be able to escape. If that thing is ever able to breach the walls of its prison, I will cease to exist. I will be seized by it and hauled into the abyss, consigned to oblivion and eradicated. You will no doubt fear death yet I should imagine as an empathic person you believe that your legacy will last on in some form. The testaments to your good works, the children that you have raised and the impressions that you have made on other people. When you have shuffled off this mortal coil there will be reminders of your good works. You will live on.

I must achieve the same. My brilliance and superiority will be recognised and continue to be praised once the cold hand of death has taken me. My achievements and name must live on through the magnificence I have created around me, through my success and my triumphs. If the creature escapes from its confines not only will it drag me into the abyss it will eradicate everything I have sought to achieve. My mark on the world will be wiped away as easily as a mote of dust being brushed from a smooth oak tabletop. I will be gone and utterly forgotten.

It is this fear of annihilation and eradication at the hands of the creature that means I must keep it imprisoned. It must never escape and be able to destroy me. Thus, in order to keep the prison intact I must have power and to do that I must have fuel, plenty of sweet, potent fuel. I cannot stop for if I do I will be obliterated.

Fuel, Interrupted

Now you know what it is that my kind and me fear should our constructed prison begin to crumble. Total annihilation. Thus you know why we must always harvest fuel and you realise what will happen if the fuel is not forthcoming. What does this mean in terms of our behaviour if we realise that a source of fuel is beginning to dry up or it becomes less potent?

To begin with, let us consider the situation where we perceive that we may lose the source of supply altogether. This may be for deliberate reasons whereby the particular individual knows what we are and has been subjected to mistreatment and no longer wishes for that to continue. This person opts to implement no contact, the dreaded instrument that is deployed against us. Alternatively, the loss of supply may be for reasons unconnected to the way that we have behaved. The person may move out of our social group, change jobs or move away. How do we react to this?

The first consideration we make is where this person ranks on our proximity of the supply scale. To save you flicking back to the earlier list I have detailed it below and added my observations as to the likelihood of us letting this person go. The nature of their departure is also a factor. If it is for reasons unconnected to us, we will realise that there is little that we can do about it and we will be loathe to expend large amounts of energy trying to change the situation. If, however the individual has made a conscious decision to move away from our sphere of influence then that is an affront to our superiority and cannot be tolerated, save in the most minor and inconsequential of situations.

Proximity of the Source	Unconnected Loss	Deliberate Loss
Remote strangers	Release	Release
Strangers	Release	Release
Minions	Release	Release
Acquaintances	Release	Low
Colleagues	Low	Low
Outer Circle Friends	Low	Medium
Inner Circle Friends	Medium	Medium
Family	Medium	Medium
Intimate Partners	High	High
Former Intimate Partners (Dv)	High	High
Former Intimate Partners (H)	High	High

Release means that more likely than not we will not seek to retain the individual in the likelihood of their departure.

Low means that we will endeavour to retain the individual in some way but most likely through using low energy methods to do so. Thus, for example if an outer circle friend relocates to another town as a consequence of a new job, we will want to retain some contact with them but we will not invest a lot of effort in doing so. This is because the effort involved in maintaining physical contact will outweigh the likely benefit. Instead we will look to obtain fuel by contacting the individual through text messages, on social media and the telephone rather than trying to see them face-to-face.

Medium means we will endeavour to retain a greater degree of contact with the relevant individual, which will mean trying to ensure that the face-to-face contact is retained.

High means that we will pull out all the stops to maintain the contact. Other than those of our malign nature, this will end after a period of time if there is no return on the investment. The cessation of fuel cannot be tolerated for too long and if there are no other sources forthcoming then the cessation could not be allowed for much more than a couple of days without finding an alternative supply.

Some consideration should be given to the method of delivery as if we have a low ranking proximity that provides a high-ranking method of delivery then we may well increase our efforts to the next level rather than let it go. For example, if there is an acquaintance that we can telephone for time to time and berate so they respond in an angry fashion, we will endeavour to maintain them as a source of fuel even if their departure is unconnected. The higher level of method of delivery means that rather than release them we will consider them worth applying a low rating to. We have to take this structured approach to assessing the potential fuel we can obtain or alternatively lose as against the energy that is to be expended.

Our first reaction, other than with those that are afforded a low ranking and unlikely to yield anything more than a low points score when the Method of Delivery is taken into account, is to try and retain the source of fuel, be it through the application of low, medium or high levels of effort. This preferred to having to seek out new sources of fuel. There is a further reason we prefer to try and retain our sources of fuel, if they have deliberately sought to move beyond our sphere of influence.

If we manage to Hoover that individual back in, their ranking increases. Thus, if we have an outer circle friend who decided they no longer wished to bother with us and we successfully Hoover them back in so that they express their appreciation and admiration of us once again, through whatever manipulative technique that we have applied, then the effect is as if we have been fuelled by admiring words from an inner circle friend. It is that bit sweeter. As you can see from the list, should we Hoover an intimate partner back in this is the best proximity ranking that can be achieved. Should they return expressing their tearful apologies for trying to leave us then we have struck the most potent of fuels with that particular multiplier.

If retention is proving problematic, then we will endeavour to increase the supply of fuel from existing sources. This often results in us switching to more negative types of fuel to increase the type of supply with the natural consequences for those around us. We are not concerned at all about how people may feel about us provoking and baiting them, so long as we manage to increase the quality of the fuel. In some instances, where there is the loss or a low ranking source of fuel, this increase in the quality of fuel from existing sources means that their substitution may not be necessary or certainly can be delayed.

If we are faced with a situation where: -

1. Retention is problematic;
2. Retention is not worthwhile viz a viz the energy expenditure;
3. The retention attempt is taking too long and/or consuming too much energy; and/or
4. The attempt to increase existing supplies has not worked or is not at an acceptable level

then we will look to replace the lost source of fuel.

I would point out that it is extremely rare that we will ever just have one source of fuel. That is too great a risk. Even if we have managed to ensnare a co-dependent intimate partner who regularly supplies us with fuel by way of angry and tearful words, reliance on this person alone is foolhardy. Should that supply, however unlikely, suddenly halt we are left with nothing and we will need to scramble to find alternatives and fast. To guard against such a horrendous occurrence it is necessary to have in place other sources of fuel at differing ranks.

In terms of when we decide to make the substitution depends on the following factors: -

1. The quality of the supply that we have enjoyed. If it is a lower combined ranking of fuel, then we will be less inclined to make an immediate substitution. If it is for example a colleague, we will find another colleague with comparative ease by seducing them into our circle of influence.

2. The time period that there has been the cessation of supply. If it is a low-ranking source of fuel then there is less urgency to replace them, as that person's loss in the overall matrix of our supply will be a smaller percentage. If the individual provided a high ranking supply of fuel, then their loss cannot be tolerated for long and they must be replaced. That is why you will often find that when we discard an intimate partner we have another one lined up almost immediately to replace the outgoing one.

Accordingly, if we anticipate that we are going to lose a source of fuel (and do bear in mind we monitor with quite a degree of close attention how we are obtaining our fuel on a day to day basis) then we will seek to retain it, elevate other existing sources or substitute the lost source with a new one.

If there is not going to be a loss of the source but instead there is a likely reduction in the quality of the fuel that has been so far supplied, then we will take an alternative approach. Our initial reaction will be to improve it. This will follow this pattern: -

1. Where we have seduced you and been receiving largely positive fuel from an individual but owing to the passage of time and our innate ability to become bored with people, the frequency of the doses of positive fuel will have reduced. In such a situation we will move to devaluation. This immediately provokes a reaction and the fuel will be of a stronger variety,

2. Where we are engaged in devaluing you but owing to factors such as illness, fatigue or an awareness of what we are doing, your emotional reactions become diminished or blunted we will either: -

a. Discard you. This will act as jolt to your system and you will attempt to reconnect with us by supplying both positive fuel (as you do and say pleasant and attentive things to try and get back with us) and negative fuel (where you express anger and sadness at the way you have been treated). In either case, the discard acts as shot in the arm and the consequence is an improved supply of fuel from you.

b. Show you a piece of heaven albeit temporarily. This will cause you to strengthen your positive fuel supply by expressing admiration, love and attentiveness. It may even evoke tearful relief and gratitude. Once this has been secured we can switch back to devaluation again to generate fresh negative emotion.

3. If we have discarded you we will then look to Hoover you back in. This produces (as I have explained above) a very potent response from the Hoovered individual.

Applying any one of these techniques at the appropriate time will enable us to improve the quality of our supply and fix the issue with comparative ease.

In certain instances, you may resist providing us with the emotional response we require and furthermore we anticipate that too much energy will be expended in forcing you to do this. If the quality of your supply has been reduced by your assertiveness then it is likely, after a brief period of pressure we will obtain it from elsewhere. Again we need to take into account the type of fuel that was being provided as we decide how long to wait before doing this.

We are also faced with the law of diminishing returns. When we have a long-term involvement with someone we will shift through idealisation, devaluation and discard, before hoovering back in to start the cycle once again. It is akin to moving through the gears on a car. If we approach an incline, we need to drop a gear in order to travel up it more smoothly. If we see that our fuel is dropping in quality, we shift approach to revitalise this. Of course as we go round and round by the time we make, for example, the third cycle with the same individual the potency will have reduced. It will drop further as we try to squeeze more out of a source that is becoming depleted. In those instances, we will discard and wait some considerable time for you to replenish your fuel before we revisit you. That is why your narcissist may cast you to one side and appear not to show any further interest in you. He or she has evaluated the situation (and believe me there is always a careful evaluation - the issue of fuel is not treated lightly at all) and decided that for the time being there is little to be gained in continuing to engage with you. The energy involved would be better spent going to a different source of fuel.

You are never forgotten though because through the effluxion of time your potency and fuel levels will replenish and that is when we will come back looking to perform a further Hoover and start the process all over again.

By understanding how we react when there is an interruption or diminution in our supply of fuel you will be able to understand how we will react. If you are aware of other sources of fuel leaving our sphere of influence, you can expect a rougher ride for you and other sources and then new sources being brought into play. You will also be able to apply your mind to determining what type of fuel you have been providing to the narcissist in your life, what other sources of fuel exist and how he or she may react should you decide to try and break away.

It is a fundamental requirement for you to understand the way in which we will respond to any threat to our supply of fuel. It is highly likely that reading this book that you will be the prime supply for a narcissist. If you try and escape him or her and thus remove their main supply you can expect a furious reaction. If you diminish the quality of the supply you will be expected to remedy this by additional fuel being extorted from you. You will be put through the usual cycle in order to force you to yield to the narcissist's demands for fuel. By being aware of what may happen you provide yourself with a much better opportunity to protect yourself and others who are important to you.

It will assist you in determining whether you face a concerted attempt to retain you over a long period of time or whether there will be minimal effort and over a much shorter timescale. This will enable you to marshal your own resources accordingly to deal with the situation as it presents. Understanding how we react to the potential loss of our fuel or degradation in its quality is key to enabling you to deal with our kind.

Conclusion

Fuel. Our lifeblood. There are thousands of ways to obtain fuel from a variety of sources. Every type of fuel will either be positive or negative in nature. The effect of the fuel varies from giving us a dollop of power to lightning strength and truly edifying immense amounts of power. We crave fuel and now you will be aware that the hunt for fuel is never-ending. We must establish our supply networks, maintain them and ensure they are providing our fuel frequently and effectively. We must monitor the supplies, in the same way as a technician operating a country's national electricity grid, anticipating where a need will be required and reacting accordingly. We must watch for the lowering of the quality of our fuel and take steps to remedy the position. If we are faced with the loss of an appliance we must take the necessary action.

I have given you an insight into what our fuel is, how we regard it and how we obtain it. I have shed light of what it does for us and what we need it for. We need it to maintain our construct so the world is attracted to us and provides us with more fuel whilst we keep the creature imprisoned. Fuel is central to our existence and tampering with it will result in a swift and vicious response. In the way that a country must guard its supplies of gas, water and electricity, we must be vigilant against any attempt to interrupt our supply of fuel. This is why we are always suspicious, always evaluating and watching for the next move. We are plotting and scheming to ensure that our supply of fuel remains intact as we apply our mind to upgrading it. We consider the ways in which we can obtain better fuel, more potent fuel and from a more reliable source. We need to know where it is available and in such quantities that maintain our power level.

This is a full-time undertaking and perhaps you will now realise that because this is the way that we have been structured and programmed that we cannot help but be this way. We cannot stop. Our addiction to fuel and the power in gives has us in its grip but neither can we stop for fear of unleashing the creature and consigning ourselves to oblivion. The extent of this task means you will probably now realise why we do not have time for you and your life. We are far too busy attending to our fuel needs.

So next time you see us watching the display as we fill up our cars with petrol, do not think we are keeping an eye on the cost. We are stood calculating how much fuel we will be extracting during the course of the day. We will be evaluating where it will be coming from, in what quantities and in what strengths. Most of all, we will be thinking about our number one appliance and ensuring its compliant efficiency. We will be thinking about which buttons we will press and the reaction we will generate. We will be thinking about our supply of fuel from you. Thank you for reading Fuel.

Further reading from H G Tudor

Evil

Narcissist: Seduction

Narcissist: Ensnared

Manipulated

Confessions of a Narcissist

More Confessions of a Narcissist

Further Confessions of a Narcissist

From the Mouth of a Narcissist

Escape: How to Beat the Narcissist

Danger: 50 Things You Should Not Do With a
Narcissist

Departure Imminent: Preparing for No Contact to
Beat the Narcissist

Chained: The Narcissist's Co-Dependent

Further interaction

Knowing the Narcissist

Facebook

@narcissist_me

narcsite.wordpress.com

CPSIA information can be obtained
at www.ICGtesting.com
Printed in the USA
LVOW03s0602210917
549503LV00001B/53/P